ADAPTING HE TEACHING FOR AN ONLINE ENVIRONMENT

RACHEL STONE AND IAN GLOVER

ADAPTING HE TEACHING FOR AN ONLINE ENVIRONMENT
// A PRACTICAL GUIDE

Los Angeles | London | New Delhi
Singapore | Washington DC | Melbourne

Los Angeles | London | New Delhi
Singapore | Washington DC | Melbourne

SAGE Publications Ltd
1 Oliver's Yard
55 City Road
London EC1Y 1SP

SAGE Publications Inc.
2455 Teller Road
Thousand Oaks, California 91320

SAGE Publications India Pvt Ltd
B 1/I 1 Mohan Cooperative Industrial Area
Mathura Road
New Delhi 110 044

SAGE Publications Asia-Pacific Pte Ltd
3 Church Street
#10-04 Samsung Hub
Singapore 049483

Editor: Amy Thornton
Senior project editor: Chris Marke
Marketing Manager: Lorna Patkai
Cover design: Wendy Scott
Typeset by: C&M Digitals (P) Ltd, Chennai, India
Printed in the UK

Library of Congress Control Number: 2021931918

British Library Cataloguing in Publication Data

A catalogue record for this book is available from
the British Library

ISBN 978-1-5297-5547-3
ISBN 978-1-5297-5548-0 (pbk)

At SAGE we take sustainability seriously. Most of our products are printed in the UK using responsibly
sourced papers and boards. When we print overseas we ensure sustainable papers are used as measured by
the PREPS grading system. We undertake an annual audit to monitor our sustainability.

CONTENTS

Acknowledgements   vi
Dedication   vii
About the Authors   ix
About this Book   x

1 What do we mean by online learning?   1

2 Creating an inclusive learning environment   11

3 Tools   22

4 Structuring online learning   34

5 Presenting online   49

6 Teaching synchronously online   62

7 Teaching asynchronously online   74

8 Assessing learning online   86

9 Further ideas and examples   101

10 Troubleshooting   112

Index   124

ACKNOWLEDGEMENTS

We would like to thank the following people for allowing us to use examples from their practice, their teaching and learning materials and sometimes even their own words in this book: Sylvia Ashton, Simon Bowles, Crispin Day, Judith Kirsch, Kate Thomas and Saskia Wilson. Thanks also to our editor Sarah Turpie, for her encouragement and her enthusiastic feedback throughout the writing process, and to Amy Thornton at Sage, for making the whole thing happen.

Thanks also to our families for the huge amount of support and encouragement (and, in some cases, childcare!) that they have provided. For Rachel, this means Reuben, Jonah, Michael, Margaret and Matthew and for Ian, Farzana and Zara.

Finally, thank you to all the participants in all the collected teaching that the two of us have carried out online over the course of our respective careers. This book is built on our experiences of developing our own practice while working with you.

To our respective children,
Jonah, Reuben and Zara

ABOUT THE AUTHORS

Rachel Stone is a Senior Lecturer in Education at Sheffield Hallam University. She has considerable experience of designing and facilitating online and blended learning in a variety of contexts, including as an e-tutor for staff employed by a fast-food chain; for Masters-level students in higher education; and as an independent consultant commissioned to produce bespoke online interactive learning materials for a range of audiences. She is also currently involved in two research projects, one on teacher belongingness in online and face-to-face environments and the other on observation and feedback in relation to teaching and learning online. Rachel is also the co-author, along with Sylvia Ashton, of *An A–Z of Creative Teaching in Higher Education*, published by Sage.

Dr Ian Glover is a Principal Learning Technologist and Senior Lecturer in the Digital Learning Team at Sheffield Hallam University and leads a team providing strategic and operational support and staff development for STEM-related departments at the university, in addition to leading strategic projects and policy development for the whole institution. His PhD research was in collaborative online learning and web annotation and he has since worked with teachers and provided academic development around the world. He has published on a wide variety of topics related to online learning.

ABOUT THIS BOOK

This short book has been written as a guide for teachers in higher education who are adapting their practice from face-to-face teaching to teaching online. It is grounded in our own combined experience and expertise in designing and facilitating online learning. Although we refer to theory at various points throughout the text, the book is very much a practical guide, not only in terms of how to move high-quality face-to-face practices online, but also how to introduce new practices that make the most of the new learning environment.

Writing this book in 2020 during a global pandemic that has required the closure of university buildings and an enforced move to majority online teaching, we are aware that many higher education practitioners have had a 'baptism of fire' in terms of the sudden shift to operating largely or even solely in a virtual environment. Over time, many have come to appreciate some of the advantages that online learning has to offer, and it is likely that universities will retain much of their online provision going forwards. In this book, therefore, we take a more measured and planned approach, focusing on how to plan online teaching and design high-quality learning experiences in the medium term, rather than providing 'quick fixes' in response to the rapid shift from face-to-face teaching that took place in 2020. However, we don't assume any prior knowledge of technology and the book is suitable for lecturers of all subject disciplines. In addition, while we are both based in a UK higher education context, we have sought to ensure that this book has global relevance by drawing on experiences of teaching and designing online learning in international contexts, as well as actively seeking to make the material widely applicable.

What about blended learning?

While writing the book we had many discussions about whether to include information about blended learning or not. We concluded that doing justice to the added complexity and choice of practices brought about by mixing online and face-to-face learning would require its own book. However, while this book is focused on developing online learning, much of the information and techniques can also be used to support the development of the online aspects of blended learning. We have not highlighted those areas which are particularly suited or unsuited to blended learning; however, all chapters contain information that can assist in creating blended learning experiences.

Structure of the book

We have structured the book so that it can be read in sequence or chapters selected as and when appropriate. If reading sequentially, the book will take you through the entire process of teaching online, from designing your online courses and activities, through selecting appropriate tools and platforms, to facilitating your teaching and assessing learning. The chapters work on a stand-alone basis too, so you can read them as they become relevant. The chapter topics are as follows.

Chapter 1 (What do we mean by online learning?) begins by looking at what we mean by 'learning online' and what makes it different from learning in a face-to-face environment. Some key terminology is introduced and we consider some of the benefits and challenges involved in designing online teaching and learning.

Chapter 2 (Creating an inclusive learning environment) addresses a topic that is fundamental to all teaching design – how to ensure that learning is inclusive and supports all learners to succeed. Here we consider some of the barriers to learning online, along with tools and approaches to ensure that the learning environment is inclusive and accessible to all.

Chapter 3 (Tools) examines the types of tools that are available to support and enhance online learning and how to make the most effective use of them. We caution against selecting technologies simply for their novelty value and look instead at how the right tools can improve student engagement and confidence.

Chapter 4 (Structuring online learning) focuses on how to plan teaching online, including making the most of the opportunities that the online environment has to offer and thinking outside the traditional linear university-based format of teaching and learning, with examples of this from practice.

Chapter 5 (Presenting online) explores ways to present knowledge in an online context, looking at asynchronous approaches (where the students access the materials in their own time). We consider lecturer presentation skills, but we also identify other ways in which to introduce new knowledge to students using some of the affordances provided by the virtual environment.

Chapter 6 (Teaching synchronously online) shines a spotlight on 'live', that is 'synchronous', teaching online, where student and teacher are present (in the virtual sense) at the same time. Considering the advantages and challenges of synchronous online teaching, we outline some of the processes of planning and facilitating effective 'real-time' learning experiences, including two contrasting case studies of different approaches.

Chapter 7 (Teaching asynchronously online) returns to the realm of asynchronous learning, identifying some group and individual online activities that can support students to develop their understanding and application of their subject discipline, and which can be undertaken completely independently at a time of their choosing.

Chapter 8 (Assessing learning online) addresses assessment and feedback approaches. When teaching online, how do you know how effectively your students are learning? How do they know themselves? Here we consider both formative and summative assessment tools, together with how to assess learning in asynchronous as well as synchronous learning contexts. The role of feedback is also considered, including how a virtual learning environment can enhance approaches to feeding back with students about their learning.

Chapter 9 (Further ideas and examples) brings many of these topics together, with some examples of creative and innovative initiatives and approaches to learning in the online environment, both 'high-tech' and 'low-tech'.

Chapter 10 (Troubleshooting) closes the book by looking at what happens when things don't go to plan, with some advice and troubleshooting techniques for both technical and non-technical issues.

Each chapter includes one or two reflective activities that are designed to help you relate the content of the book to your own teaching context, providing opportunities to engage in planning and designing your own high-quality online learning experiences for your students.

Further information

Additional material to supplement the contents of this book is available at www.adaptingteaching.com

1

WHAT DO WE MEAN BY ONLINE LEARNING?

CHAPTER SUMMARY

We begin with some examples of online learning and invite the reader to consider similar experiences of their own. We then introduce some key vocabulary before examining the process of designing online learning, taking account of some of the pros and cons of this medium. A reflective task analysing an existing course and the challenges and opportunities of adapting it for an online environment follows, with a case study and analysis to finish.

Introduction

> **REFLECTIVE ACTIVITY 1.1**
>
> Think of something you learned recently online. Here are some examples:
>
> - how to find and restore a 'Minecraft' world that your child accidentally deleted;
> - which extinguishers you should use for which type of fire, as part of the fire safety training course at your place of work;
> - how to cut your own hair;
> - how compound interest affects long-term savings and debts;
> - the historical accuracy of the costumes in the musical *Hamilton*;
> - how to manage an existing health condition (using, for example, the UK National Health Service website).
>
> How effectively did you learn the thing that you set out to learn? What helped? What didn't?

Thoughts

The word 'learning' comes from 'lernen' in Old High German, meaning 'following' or 'finding the track' (Harper, 2001–20). This seems to reflect something of how learning can occur online in the twenty-first century, in the sense that teaching online is about designing or finding resources that enable the learner to 'find their way', often by themselves, in their own time.

So, if 'learning' is about finding one's way, then a large part of the teacher's role must involve creating the right opportunities, resources and skills development support for the learning to take place. This is perhaps why Laurillard (2012: 1) calls teaching a 'design science', like engineering or architecture, where designs are created for a particular purpose, building on what is already known. This is a long way from teaching being about placing yourself in front of a group of students and simply telling them what you know. Designing *teaching* involves setting intended learning aims and outcomes and then developing or sourcing materials and/or activities that will support the learner to reach them. In an online environment, there is a wealth of tools available for just that purpose.

Going back to the list of examples above (including your own), there are some apparent differences in the ways in which online learning takes place. On the one hand, topics such as employer-led fire safety training, learning about compound interest and finding out how to manage a health condition from a government website are likely to involve bespoke resources that have been professionally designed with the aim of enabling learning to occur on a fixed topic. Managing Minecraft worlds, finding out how to cut your own hair and researching the costume design of a historical musical, on the other hand, are more likely to involve a search on the internet, an assessment of appropriate sources of information and a selection from those available, including discussion forums, home-made videos and blogs. This requires a reasonable level of web-literacy and the ability to critique a range of sources of knowledge. If you are planning to move a face-to-face course or module to an online environment, you will need to consider the nature of the resources available, which are the best 'fit' in terms of supporting the learners to achieve the intended outcomes and what skills and guidance your students will need in order to access them.

There are differences in the drivers for learning as well. Some examples of online learning involve spontaneous, self-initiated activity, while others require the learner to follow instructions. Opportunities for learner interaction are also varied. Some activities could involve dialogue such as an exchange of ideas, or a multiple-choice quiz to test recall, while other examples might require the learner only to read or watch what has been presented. It is important to explore the research into online learning in your own subject discipline in this respect. For example, in modern foreign languages it has been shown that social interaction between peers (via media such as online language learning marketplaces) enhances academic performance (Al-Hasan, 2021). However, other research indicates that people of different cultural backgrounds can vary widely in terms of the importance that they attach to 'social presence' in an online environment (Gunawardena and Jayatilleke, 2014), so a strategy for encouraging social presence would need to be carefully designed. Another study (Su and Waugh, 2018), in the context of postgraduate science, suggests that managing expectations, providing flexibility and maintaining regular human contact can all help to minimise attrition rates and prevent students from disengaging. We will return to research findings such as these as we look at different aspects of online learning in the rest of this book.

One of the differences between online learning and face-to-face teaching is that when the teacher is physically present they can act as a mitigating factor in terms of some of these aspects; for example, they can provide motivation, explain difficult texts and troubleshoot any issues arising, perhaps with on-site IT support. With online learning, however, even when the teacher is present online and the learning is taking place in real time, aspects such as learner motivation, the availability and quality of resources, addressing the digital capabilities of the students and ensuring access to the necessary equipment and connectivity need to be planned and accounted for in much greater detail and depth. With face-to-face learning, the teacher is in the boat with the students, steering the course. With online learning, the students are scattered out on the waters in their own vessels and the teacher must guide them from a distance. Preparation is therefore essential, not simply in terms of learning content and media but also in relation to building a community and enabling students to feel supported.

By now, we hope, you will have begun to realise that online learning is not something that can be treated as 'equivalent' to face-to-face learning (although there are some similarities), and that online teaching involves more than a simple 'screen-dump' of all your face-to-face resources, slides and videos. The rest of this book is designed to take you through the process of planning teaching and learning for an online environment.

Terminology

We have, so far, contrasted 'online' learning with 'face-to-face' learning, but, before proceeding further, we need to clarify the meaning of these and other terms.

Online learning, for the authors of this book, means learning via the medium of the internet, through a device such as a laptop, personal computer, tablet or smartphone. This is most commonly done from home, but could in fact take place anywhere.

Face-to-face learning, in this book, means learning in an environment where the teacher and the students are physically present, within sight and hearing of each other. In higher education (HE) this is sometimes referred to as 'on-campus' learning. Neither term is entirely accurate; for example, students and teacher may be 'face to face' in an online video-conferencing session, or students may be engaging in online learning while 'on campus', perhaps in the university library. But unless otherwise stated, 'face-to-face' and 'on-campus' mean here that the learning is taking place in a geographical location where both teacher and students are in attendance in person.

Digital learning means learning with the aid of electronic equipment. It encompasses online learning but also includes, for example, students using mobile phones in a lecture theatre, say to vote on a question posed by the lecturer.

Blended learning, however, encompasses a learning experience that involves both face-to-face and online learning. For example, the students might complete most of their learning online, but come into the university for one day a week for tutorials and seminars. This type of learning is becoming increasingly common in the sector. In this book, we focus on the 'online' part of the learning, but it is worth pointing out that in a blended programme both aspects need careful planning, along with the transitions between face-to-face and online content.

Distance learning is learning that takes place remotely, with the learner and teacher in different physical locations. Much of the learning is likely to take place online, but it might also encompass the mailing out of paper-based workbooks or learning packs, telephone tutorials and the postal submission of assignments and feedback.

Synchronous online learning takes place on a specified date, at a specified time. The teacher and the students are all online together, and the teaching takes place 'live', in real time. This type of online learning is explored further in Chapter 6.

Asynchronous online learning can be accessed by students at a time of their own choosing. This type of learning involves self-access resources such as slides, audio files, videos, quizzes or online research tasks, which the student can engage with at their own pace. Students may be required to submit a piece of work to evidence their engagement with the resources, or post a comment on a discussion board, either individually or as part of a small group. We look at asynchronous online learning in Chapter 7.

Designing online teaching and learning

Digital technologies trigger a different kind of relationship between the teacher, the learners, and what is being learned.

(Laurillard, 2013)

There is a temptation to think of technology as simply another type of tool to aid teaching and learning, in the same way as books or chalkboards. To a certain extent this is true, but this does not mean that technological tools should dictate the nature of the learning; nor should they be employed purely for their own novelty value (Glover *et al.*, 2016). Beetham and Sharpe (2013) argue that new technologies in the so-called 'Digital Age' have transformed the nature of knowledge in society and thus the nature of learning itself. This means appreciating 'where digital technologies have the potential to disrupt norms, challenge assumptions, innovate disciplines and professions, and usher in completely new forms of learning activity' (2013: 4). We explore this further in Chapters 3 and 4.

There are other factors to consider in designing online education, some of which can be exploited and others which need to be mitigated against.

Some advantages of learning online

The flexibility afforded by learning online means that it can often be more effective than face-to-face learning. This is because students can learn at their own pace, repeating some material and skipping through other parts (Li and Lalani, 2020). They can also learn when and where they choose, meaning that students from different countries can take part (De Paepe et al., 2018).

The non-linearity of online education is also a plus, along with access to a vast range of resources, while the multimodal nature of the materials can make learning more fun (Koutsoupidou, 2014). Of course, all of this is dependent on the programme and materials design, including the range and variety of the learning activities on offer. The rest of this book contains a multitude of examples.

Some of the challenges of learning online

These are addressed in more detail in Chapter 10, but a brief summary is given here.

Some students who lack the appropriate equipment or reliable internet access may struggle to participate (Li and Lalani, 2020). There may be technical problems for some in accessing the course materials (Blake, 2013), while others may lack the digital capability needed (De Paepe et al., 2018). All these factors should be taken into account when designing online programmes.

A further barrier is the sense of isolation that some learners can experience in relation to the online environment, as well as feeling distanced from the tutor (De Paepe et al., 2018). Teaching staff themselves may be in need of training to improve their own digital literacy, and closing the gap between learner and teacher requires a multi-pronged approach in an online environment, including tutor 'presence' and multiple opportunities for interaction (Wagner, 2020).

One factor that plays a big role in determining the success or failure of an online learning programme is the mindset of the stakeholders involved (O'Doherty et al., 2018). Rather than being the 'poor cousin' of face-to-face learning, online education provides a wealth of possibilities and opportunities, many of which are explored in this book. A positive attitude and an open mind can therefore go a long way.

REFLECTIVE ACTIVITY 1.2: ADAPTING A FACE-TO-FACE COURSE FOR AN ONLINE ENVIRONMENT

Consider a course or module that you teach currently in a face-to-face format and begin to consider the implications of changing the mode of delivery into an online one. Complete a chart such as the one shown (Table 1.1). This forms the basis of what is known as a 'SWOT' analysis. (If you have never attempted a SWOT analysis before, see Orr (2013) for more on this approach. There is also an example of one in Table 1.2 below.)

Table 1.1   SWOT analysis template

Title of course:	
Number of students:	
Duration and current delivery pattern of course:	
Other information (e.g. work placements, lab sessions):	
Adapting the course for an online learning environment	
Strengths	**Opportunities**
Weaknesses	**Threats**

Case Study

Table 1.2 shows an example of a part of SWOT analysis for a teacher education course.

Table 1.2   An example SWOT analysis for a teacher education course

Title of course: *Teaching Skills for Doctoral Students*	
Number of students: *3 cohorts of 30 students, taught at different points in the year*	
Duration of course: *6 weeks, ½ a day per week face-to-face contact. Directed tasks set each week*	
Other information: *Non-accredited but certificate of attendance available*	
Adapting the course for an online learning environment	
Strengths	**Opportunities**
• *well-established course* • *existing course site on the university virtual learning environment with all the materials* • *students IT-literate and working at doctoral level* • *university has learning technologists who can help with learning design*	• *some funding available to convert face-to-face materials into online-friendly formats* • *university supports several different tools for online learning* • *can model good practice in online teaching, which will benefit the participants*

(Continued)

Table 1.2   (Continued)

Weaknesses	Threats
• *course is popular because of its success in building a learning community of students of different disciplines (and also nationalities) – more of a challenge online* • *limited amount of time in which to prepare the online version* • *current content needs updating* • *some members of the teaching team not confident in use of digital technology*	• *students are completing their own doctorates and some have graduate teaching assistant roles, which means competing demands on their time – attrition rate may be high* • *course may not be as popular in an online format, so may struggle to recruit participants*

From the SWOT analysis extract, the following points are apparent in relation to the course described (we go into more detail about how these might be addressed in Chapter 4).

- **Time for planning and preparation is limited**, so either the start date will need to be delayed or the online adaptation process will need to be staged.
- **The students currently appreciate the opportunity to get to know others outside their own immediate departments**. For an online course, this social aspect of learning needs careful planning.
- **Without scheduled face-to-face sessions, some students may find it hard to prioritise the time needed to engage with the course** (although, as mentioned, online learning may suit others better due to its flexible nature). We look at ways of addressing this in Chapter 10.

From this exercise, it is clear that the transition from face-to-face teaching to the facilitation of online learning is not a straightforward one. Conducting an analysis such as this enables planning and preparation procedures to be put into place so that not only is the process made manageable, but also all aspects are considered and a learning environment is created that is inclusive and supportive.

Further reading

Kurt, S. (2018) TPACK: technological pedagogical content knowledge framework. *Educational Technology*, 12 May. Available online at: educationaltechnology.net/technological-pedagogical-content-knowledge-tpack-framework/ (accessed 27 August 2020).

Looks at the challenges teachers have in engaging in digital learning technology due to gaps in their own knowledge.

Martin, F., Stamper, B. and Flowers, C. (2020) Examining student perception of readiness for online learning: importance and confidence. *Online Learning*, 24(2).

Study showing that students were much more confident in online attributes and technical competence than in time management and communication skills.

Richardson, J., Besser, E., Koehler, A., Lim, J. and Strait, M. (2016) Instructors' perceptions of instructor presence in online learning environments. *International Review of Research in Open and Distance Learning*, 17(4), 82–104.

Multiple case-study enquiry exploring teachers' online 'presence' on an e-learning Masters course and the potential impact on students.

References

Al-Hasan, A. (2021) Effects of social network information on online language learning performance: a cross-continental experiment. *International Journal of e-Collaboration*, 17(2), 1–16.

Beetham, H. and Sharpe, R. (eds) (2013) *Rethinking Pedagogy for a Digital Age: Designing for 21st Century Learning*. Abingdon: Routledge.

Blake, R.J. (2013) *Brave New Digital Classroom: Technology and Foreign Language Learning*. Washington, DC: Georgetown University Press.

De Paepe, L., Zhu, C. and Depryck, K. (2018) Online Dutch L2 learning in adult education: educators' and providers' viewpoints on needs, advantages and disadvantages. *Open Learning: The Journal of Open, Distance and e-Learning*, 33(1), 18–33.

Glover, I., Hepplestone, S., Parkin, H., Rodger, H. and Irwin, B. (2016) Pedagogy first: realising technology enhanced learning by focusing on teaching practice. *British Journal of Educational Technology*, 47(5), 993–1002.

Gunawardena, C.N. and Jayatilleke, B.G. (2014) Facilitating online learning and cross-cultural e-mentoring. In Jung, I. and Gunawardena, C. (eds), *Culture and Online Learning : Global Perspectives and Research*. Sterling, Vancouver: Stylus, LLC. Chapter 7, 67–78.

Harper, D. (2001–20) Learn. *Etymology Dictionary*. Online at https://www.etymonline.com/word/learn (accessed 26 August 2020).

Koutsoupidou, T. (2014) Online distance learning and music training: benefits, drawbacks and challenges. *Open Learning: The Journal of Open, Distance and e-Learning*, 29(3), 243–55.

Laurillard, D. (2012) *Teaching as a Design Science: Building Pedagogical Patterns for Learning and Technology*. Abingdon: Routledge.

Laurillard, D. (2013) Foreword to the second edition. In Beetham, H. and Sharpe, R. (eds), *Rethinking Pedagogy for a Digital Age: Designing for 21st Century Learning*. Abingdon: Routledge. xvi–xviii.

Li, C. and Lalani, F. (2020) The COVID-19 pandemic has changed education forever. This is how. *World Economic Forum*. 29 April. Available online at: https://www.weforum.org/agenda/2020/04/coronavirus-education-global-covid19-online-digital-learning/ (accessed 6 September 2020).

O'Doherty, D., Dromey, M., Lougheed, J., Hannigan, A., Last, J. and McGrath, D. (2018) Barriers and solutions to online learning in medical education: an integrative review. *BMC Medical Education*, 18(1), 130.

Orr, B. (2013) Conducting a SWOT analysis for program improvement. *US–China Education Review*. A, 3(6), 381.

Su, J. and Waugh, M.L. (2018) Online student persistence or attrition: observations related to expectations, preferences, and outcomes. *Journal of Interactive Online Learning*, 16(1), 63–79.

Wagner, V. (2020) Classroom of the future: the rise of online learning. *E-Commerce Times*. 14 May. Available online at: https://www.ecommercetimes.com/story/86666.html (accessed 6 September 2020).

2

CREATING AN INCLUSIVE
LEARNING ENVIRONMENT

CHAPTER SUMMARY

Possible barriers to an individual achieving their full potential in higher education, or even taking part at all, are many. However, with thought and planning we can reduce the negative impact of these. In this chapter we will look at some issues related to accessibility that affect how people with disabilities and impairments can use online information, or even whether they can at all. We will also take a brief look at some other considerations when developing inclusive learning environments. Addressing these issues results in a more inclusive learning experience that benefits all learners.

Introduction

According to Hockings (2010: 1), 'inclusive learning and teaching in higher education refers to the ways in which pedagogy, curricula and assessment are designed to engage students in learning that is meaningful, relevant, and accessible to all'. As educators we are passionate about our discipline and sharing that enthusiasm with our students. However, while most of us would instinctively agree that education should be available to all and are increasingly aware of how government decisions can encourage or dissuade people from study, we often do not consider how the smaller decisions that we make about our teaching and materials can do the same. Fortunately, while as individuals we have little influence on national policy, we can adjust our own teaching and influence that of our colleagues to be as inclusive as possible.

The principle of valuing diversity means that inclusivity is a very broad topic that encompasses topics such as disability; colonialism and race; gender and sexuality; age; work and family responsibilities; and class and socioeconomics. In this chapter we focus on people's ability to access and use learning materials online, though other aspects of accessibility are also introduced.

Accessibility

Legislative drive for accessibility

Several countries have now introduced legislation that mandates online material meet accessibility standards to increase inclusivity. For example, in 2018 the United Kingdom introduced laws that require all online material produced by public sector bodies, including universities and colleges, to meet the Web Content Accessibility Guidelines (WCAG) 2.1 standards.

This legislation has led to software companies developing their products to be compliant with the standards – for example, by incorporating tools to help you check your materials. This means that a large part of the standards are met for you automatically when using compliant software, so you just need to focus on the specific accessibility of your materials.

SCULPT model

To help their staff with developing accessible materials, the UK's Worcestershire County Council has developed a simple model that emphasises six basic elements to consider: the SCULPT model (http://www.worcestershire.gov. uk/sculpt, accessed 27 August 2020). Due to its simplicity and practicality, SCULPT is being adopted by a growing number of other public bodies, including several universities.

The SCULPT model comprises:

- **Structure** – use heading styles and ensure text flows in the right order on slides and documents;
- **Colour and contrast** – colours selected to maximise contrast and not convey information;
- **Use of images** – add descriptive 'alternative' text and avoid solely using images to provide information;
- **Links** – make sure text used for links is meaningful and informative, not 'click here' or full web address;
- **Plain English** – avoid jargon and use simple, unambiguous language wherever possible;
- **Table structure** – use only simple table structures.

Figure 2.1 shows how some of these principles can be applied to improve a set of slides. No useful information has been lost, but the simplified images, structure and fonts make the slides more accessible for all.

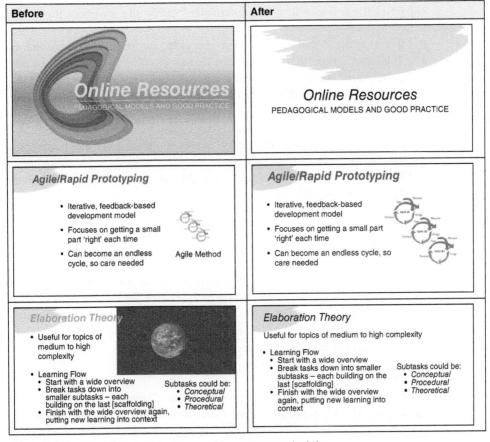

Figure 2.1   Slides before and after applying SCULPT principles

While a simple set of guidelines, applying the SCULPT model can make a huge difference to accessibility and largely address the WCAG 2.1 standards. Although applying the model to existing materials is additional effort, once you start using the model when creating new materials it is likely that it will speed up your creative process.

Accessibility for video

SCULPT works well for text-based materials, but there is a growing area of educational materials that it does not address directly: video. Video can be a very effective and engaging method of teaching, particularly when used to demonstrate processes or show historic events. It is also increasingly popular for making resources to replace content-heavy teaching, such as lectures.

Video can be a difficult type of material to make more accessible because it is both a visual and an auditory medium, meaning that it can present challenges to students with visual impairments and those with hearing impairments. However, there are relatively simple ways to reduce the impact of these issues that will potentially benefit all viewers of the video:

1. If the platform used to distribute the video supports captions, such as YouTube, ensure that they are enabled and, where possible, review and correct any automatically generated captions.
2. Ensure that you audibly describe any relevant visual information, such as graphs or images.
3. Similarly, if there is a particularly important piece of audio, such as a piece of music being played or a sound effect, add the name or a description of it to the captions.
4. If you wrote a script or notes to use during recording the video, share them alongside the video.

Accessibility tools

As every person has different requirements there are a wide variety of accessibility tools available, many of which are free for anyone to use. Even if you do not personally need to use any of these tools, it is well worth trying some out for a few hours to get an understanding of how your students may access and perceive electronic information.

Screen readers
These read out the text and software interface elements that are displayed on screen, allowing people with visual impairments to hear electronic

documents and navigate around the computer. The two most widely used dedicated screen readers are JAWS (https://support.freedomscientific.com/JAWSHQ/JAWSHeadquarters01, accessed 27 August 2020) and NVDA (https://www.nvaccess.org/); these can produce braille as well as audio. Basic screen-reading features are provided with Windows ('Narrator') and MacOS ('VoiceOver').

While screen readers are now quite effective when working with most documents that have a relatively simple structure, they struggle to read out mathematical formulae in a meaningful way. This is a significant barrier for people with visual impairments when studying a wide range of STEM subjects. Fortunately, there are additional tools that can work with JAWS and NVDA to better read out mathematical equations, with JAWS supporting the widely used LaTeX typesetting language and NVDA working with MathPlayer (https://www.dessci.com/en/products/mathplayer/download.htm, accessed 27 August 2020) to support the web-based MathML markup language.

Dictation

Dictation software is also available and can be used by students to speak their words rather than type them. While previously requiring specialist software, the functionality is now being built into common software such as Microsoft Word. This can be a very good way for students with dyslexia, motor impairments and visual impairments to produce text efficiently. Where these once required significant amounts of configuration to get accurate results, the latest versions make use of servers on the internet to get good accuracy immediately. In fact, this entire paragraph was dictated into Word and did not require any corrections! It is important to recognise that when students use this technology, their work may be more speech-like than those who are typing directly into the computer.

Alternative formats

Alternative formats may be better suited to an individual's needs than the standard ones, such as text provided as an audio file or a format that works better with the individual's assistive technology. Tools are available that can convert between different formats when requested by the students, for example Blackboard Ally (https://ally.ac/), and these allow students to obtain files in a format that works for them with no need for the tutor to convert the files manually.

It is important to remember that in most jurisdictions there are copyright exceptions that allow an individual to convert between formats for accessibility purposes. However, these exceptions do not apply to tutors pre-emptively making more accessible versions of copyrighted material for their students, unless they have a specific licence to do so, so the student will typically need to explicitly request the alternative format for themselves.

While PDF has been recommended as a 'print-equivalent' file format for distributing materials to students for some time, it is less suitable as an accessible format than other file types. In fact, due to the new accessibility features and the ability to change font sizes, background colours, etc., the docx format used by Word is now seen as a more accessible option. A further issue affecting PDF files is when the PDF is made by scanning an existing document, as these often consist of an image of each of the pages that cannot be read by screen reader software. In these situations, a new version of the PDF should be produced that contains the actual text, not just a scanned image, or an updated version should be sourced through the library.

Checking accessibility

In addition to tools and methods used by people to access information, there are tools to help creators of information to produce materials that are more accessible from the start. Some very useful ones are:

- the Accessibility checker built into recent versions of Microsoft Office packages, such as Word and PowerPoint, which can identify and help fix common problems;
- Blackboard Ally which, in addition to creating more accessible formats, can also check files in a similar way to the Office tools and suggest ways to make them more accessible;
- Colorblinding (https://chrome.google.com/webstore/detail/colorblinding/dgbgleaofjainknadoffbjkclicbbgaa?hl=en), an extension for the Chrome web browser that can simulate different types of colour blindness and allow you to see if there are potential problems with the colours that you are using.

REFLECTIVE ACTIVITY 2.1

- Pick a document or web resource that you have created and that is typical of your materials.
- Use a screen reader to read it to you.
- Apply the principles of the SCULPT model to it.
- Use the screen reader on the amended version – is it easier to understand and follow than the original?

For further information on accessibility, AbilityNet (https://abilitynet.org.uk), a UK-based charity, provides guidance, support and consultancy related to making technology accessible to people with a wide variety of conditions and impairments.

Other inclusivity considerations

In addition to accessibility, there are other considerations and design decisions that affect the inclusiveness of a learning experience. Quite often, the inclusivity of online learning is negatively affected by making assumptions about the students based on experience of more traditional, face-to-face learning situations. However, this can be improved by thinking about the differences between these two modes of learning and teaching and how they can affect and enable student learning.

Technical barriers

While students on campus will generally have unlimited access to high-speed wireless internet provided by the university and high-spec computers with the necessary software for their studies, individuals may not have, or be able to afford, equivalent equipment to assist their studies off-campus. These barriers can be reduced by thinking about the software and activities that students will need to use as part of their studies and identifying where software can be provided to students and lower cost or less resource-intensive alternatives can be used. For example, rather than providing recordings in Ultra High Definition 4k resolution it may be that lower resolution video will be just as useful yet work on lower specification computers and over slower or data-capped internet connections.

Resource availability

Similar to technology availability outlined above, it is important to ensure that students can access the necessary supplementary materials from where they are. This means that books that are only available in physical form from the university library should be replaced by alternatives that are available electronically wherever possible.

Digital capability

Learning online generally requires a higher level of skill and confidence with using technology for both students and tutors. It is important to introduce new technologies carefully to allow people to develop confidence with their use. Also, while it is tempting to think that younger people will have higher levels of digital capability than older ones, it is not necessarily the case, and they certainly may not have much experience of using digital tools to support their studies rather than for social purposes.

Multiple time zones

When students are studying entirely online, there is the potential for them to reside in other countries. This can create difficulties in attending live sessions when the time difference is taken into account, such as a 4 p.m. session starting at midnight for students in a time zone that is eight hours ahead, or a 9 a.m. session being at 1 a.m. for someone eight hours behind. Ideally, sessions would be planned to allow all students to take part at a reasonable local time; however, it may become necessary to cluster students based on time zone and run live sessions multiple times, once per cluster.

Use of social media

As social media becomes more integrated with learning and teaching it is important to recognise that this might act as a barrier to participation for students who do not want to share personal information with commercial companies or do not want to share their thoughts and opinions publicly. Therefore, it is important to think about what can be done to allow these students to participate fully while maintaining their privacy. For example, perhaps the students could sign up under a pseudonym or multiple students share a single account. There may also be issues with students even accessing the social media platform from some countries, such as Twitter being blocked in China. Inability to take part in the social media activities could present a significant barrier and reduce inclusivity in these cases. The use of social media is discussed further in Chapter 3.

Work and family commitments

Moving to online learning can allow a wider range of people to take part because they can study alongside other commitments where full-time, face-to-face study would not be possible. However, this means that it is important to consider these other time commitments, such as by maintaining a regular pattern of activity and by giving students enough time to complete activities even when they are juggling their other work and family requirements. Many online learning tools will also provide statistics that can be used to check the engagement level of individual students, allowing tutors to identify potential issues and contact students to follow up and provide support.

While the above points are extremely relevant to online learning, there are more generic aspects of inclusivity that relate just as much to face-to-face learning as online learning.

Decolonising the curriculum

The heritage of 'Western higher' education, and the assumption of European cultural superiority that itself fuelled and resulted from the Imperial age, has led to a bias towards White, Anglo-European thinkers, writers and theorists with little-to-no representation of schools of thought and practice from other cultures and parts of the world. This blind spot is a problem for all students, but for those whose heritage is not White European it can appear that the subject is not for 'people like them' and that their own cultural heritage is worth less than those who are represented (Charles, 2019). While it may be easier to address this problem in some subjects, such as by integrating work by black and minority ethnic (BAME) writers, artists, historians and scientists, for others it may be more difficult. However, it is also possible to bring diversity into the teaching by changing the focus of the applied aspects of the materials – for example, instead of case studies looking at public healthcare in Dublin, Durham or Detroit, can you use Dubai, Durban, or Delhi? Rather than an assessment to design a green transport network for Huddersfield, would one for Hanoi be possible?

Prior knowledge and experience

People tend to think about groups of people as a single mass with a common set of knowledge and experience, rather than as a collection of individuals each with their own unique set of knowledge and experience. While this can make it easier to engage with most of the group, those who do not conform to that stereotype may feel marginalised. For example, will a student from Canada or China have the context and knowledge to understand what you mean when you make an analogy based on a TV programme only popular in the UK?

Challenging the tutor

Some cultures instil such respect for the authority of the tutor that students will not question what they are told (Merriam and Kim, 2008). This can be a problem in situations where the tutor is deliberately taking an incorrect or controversial position to challenge the students. It should therefore be explained that this is role-play and that students are expected to challenge what is being said.

Social anxiety

Due to natural inclination, cultural reasons or mental health issues, some students may feel particularly anxious about speaking in front of their peers, sometimes to the point that they will stop attending sessions where they might have to contribute (Cohen *et al.*, 2019). Other students may prefer to think deeply before committing to an answer and feel uncomfortable if put on the spot. It is important to respect these differences while allowing all to take part. For example, you could allow anonymous discussions online, make the activity asynchronous to give more time for thinking or allow students to discuss in small groups before providing a collective response.

REFLECTIVE ACTIVITY 2.2

- Consider a learning activity that you use with your students.
- What assumptions does it make about your students, such as how, when and where they will take part in the activities, their language and technical ability, or external commitments?
- Redesign the activity to remove or reduce these assumptions and make it more inclusive.
- Try your amended activity on someone else and get some feedback.

Further reading

The Public Sector Bodies (Websites and Mobile Applications) (No. 2) Accessibility Regulations 2018: https://www.legislation.gov.uk/uksi/2018/952/contents/made (accessed 27 August 2020).

At the time of writing, the current UK accessibility legislation covering universities and other public sector organisations.

WCAG 2.1 at a Glance: https://www.w3.org/WAI/standards-guidelines/wcag/glance/ (accessed 27 August 2020).

A brief summary of the Web Content Accessibility Guidelines, version 2.1, that are the basis of many countries' minimum accessibility requirements.

References

Charles, E. (2019) Decolonizing the curriculum. *Insights*, 32(1), 24. DOI: http://doi.org/10.1629/uksg.475

Cohen, M., Buzinski, S.G., Armstrong-Carter, E., Clark, J., Buck, B. and Reuman, L. (2019) Think, pair, freeze: the association between social anxiety and student discomfort in the active learning environment. *Scholarship of Teaching and Learning in Psychology*, 5(4), 265–77. DOI: https://doi.org/10.1037/stl0000147

Hockings, C. (2010) *Inclusive Learning and Teaching in Higher Education: A Synthesis of Research*. York: Higher Education Academy.

Merriam, S.B. and Kim, Y.S. (2008) Non-Western perspectives on learning and knowing. *New Directions for Adult and Continuing Education*. 71–81. DOI: http://10.1002/ace.307

3

TOOLS

CHAPTER SUMMARY

In this chapter we look at how to embrace technology in a way that supports our aims and identify some of the technologies currently being used to enhance learning. We also consider a couple of problems that can be faced when introducing technology into teaching: allowing the technology to define the teaching; and avoiding using a technology until long after it has shown to be valuable. We finish with a case study showing how appropriate use of technology has improved student confidence on placement and, potentially, enhanced employability.

Introduction

This chapter is about tools, but what do we mean by 'tools'? 'Tool' is broadly synonymous with 'technology' in this context; the reason for picking the term 'tool' is that we feel it makes explicit the fact that these are things that assist in doing something – a 'tool' isn't an abstract concept or a hyped new product, it is the thing that helps you bang a nail into a wall, cut food into pieces that fit your mouth, or, in our case here, helps teachers teach and learners learn. As Beetham and Sharpe point out:

> there is nothing new about technologies for learning. Papyrus and paper, chalk and print, overhead projectors, educational toys and television, even the basic technologies of writing were innovations once. [All have been] assimilated to pedagogical practice without altering the fundamental truths about how people learn.

> (2007: 4)

We will be using both words in this chapter, but generally use 'tool' to refer to something with clear practical uses and 'technology' for those larger concepts and categories.

The temptation of techno-determinism

When applying technology to teaching, it is very easy to allow the technology to lead and define the teaching – a situation sometimes called 'techno-determinism' (Kirkwood, 2015). This is particularly the case when a new, hyped technology appears and ways to make use of it in teaching are sought. For example, when iPads first appeared there were many attempts to shoe-horn them into teaching due to thinking that their novelty would engage the students, rather than considering what the students were learning and how the specific features of an iPad could enhance that learning. A more recent example in higher education is virtual reality (VR) – immersive, synthetic experiences that use a headset to place the user in a 3D world. Unfortunately, while it is possible to create the innovative, engaging and highly educational experiences used to promote VR, this requires both a range of advanced specialist skills and a significant amount of time to produce. In addition, the immersive nature of VR means that the experience can quickly become frustrating as the user finds the boundaries of what is possible in the software, which then detracts from the actual learning.

Allowing the technology on offer to determine the mode of learning is very tempting as a way to 'spice up' teaching and learning for both the teacher and the student by introducing new tools and approaches into the experience, but it can have severe pitfalls. The main potential problem is that, without very careful planning, the innovation may just be a gimmick that provides no benefit to learning or, worse, requires such a significant amount of time spent learning the tool that it reduces the amount of time spent on using it to learn the subject.

A further issue with being at the 'cutting edge' of technology is that it may be detrimental to creating an inclusive learning environment, as discussed in Chapter 2, due to potentially requiring students to own or have access to more powerful computers or tablets, and the possibility of the innovative tools not having been designed for use by people with specific disabilities or those who lack a high level of technical expertise. For example, the 'Design' feature in MS PowerPoint can create impressive-looking slides with great images, but with text that is far too small for some students to read.

The lure of laggardism

The flipside of the above is resisting using technology and new approaches for as long as possible, potentially until they have become so widely used that they are essentially already the baseline and therefore viewed as already being stale. In his Diffusion of Innovation model, Rogers (2003) would classify such people as 'Laggards'. While this term has negative connotations, an alternative that better expresses the mindset of this group is 'Traditionalist'.

The Laggard is highly risk-averse and lets others try out new tools and approaches, prove their value and work through all issues before they even consider adoption. However, even when the value of these tools and ideas has been widely proven, it often takes external pressure for the Laggard to change their practice. This attitude can be very alluring because it allows the Laggard to stay within their comfort zone. Ultimately, however, this mindset is problematic for the students as they may be missing out on approaches that might enhance their learning. While in some cases being a Laggard is an explicit choice, for many people it is the result of technophobia or the fear of losing credibility with students should the technology not work perfectly. In both these cases the fear is typically larger than the reality and building a little confidence to try something new, perhaps with the support of a learning technologist at your institution, is the first step.

Thinking pedagogically about technology

To avoid falling into either of the above traps it is necessary to think pedagogically rather than technologically. Instead, follow the usual process for designing teaching, such as identifying your intended learning outcomes and then identifying what tools are available that can most effectively enable your students to achieve these (Glover *et al.*, 2016). When thinking about tools that can enhance your students' learning, a further consideration is to coordinate with colleagues also teaching these students to ensure that students aren't unnecessarily having to learn multiple tools for the same purpose simply because different teachers prefer different tools. This coordination will likely mean that compromises need to be made but it will ultimately benefit the students by reducing confusion and letting them focus on learning.

All of this is not to say that you should never introduce new tools and approaches into your teaching – if no one did then practice would be stagnant. Rather, you should be guided by the pedagogy and intended learning in selecting where it would be appropriate to do so. For example, introducing an essentially untested tool into a high-stakes assessment would be extremely ill-advised, but using it in a low-stakes activity would allow the benefits and drawbacks to be investigated while not jeopardising the students' learning.

When considering tools that might support and enhance your practice, wherever possible you should first look at those provided and supported by your institution rather than simply selecting a tool yourself, since:

- the institution will provide support and training for such tools;
- they will have been checked for legal issues such as data protection and accessibility compliance;
- they may have additional features to any free version; and
- user accounts may have been set up.

This is not to say that non-institutional tools should never be used – they may be the best or only option for the task – but that they should be investigated prior to use. Where possible, you should discuss your plans to use an external tool with learning technologists at your institution because they may know how the tool is already being used, including any issues or limitations, and be able to investigate practical and legal implications for you. At Sheffield Hallam University we worked with teachers from across all disciplines to produce a *Teaching Approaches Menu* (Sheffield Hallam University, 2014) that aligns pedagogical approaches used at the institution with technologies shown to be effective with our students (Figure 3.1). This *Menu* has been adopted by other universities so it may be that your institution has something similar tailored for your context.

When selecting tools to use in online learning it is important to think at the level of an individual activity ('micro'), the module level ('meso') and the overall course level ('macro') to create a consistent experience for the students. Some variety in tools is, however, desirable. For example, when web-based polling tools started to appear they were seen as a relatively easy way for teachers to gauge the understanding of their students during

	Approaches to teaching and learning	Benefits	Indicative assessment artefacts	Technology to support and enhance
Information-focused Learning	**Lectures as pre-work (a.k.a. 'Flipped Classroom)** *Information and lectures provided as pre-work, contact time used for more interactive purposes*	• Students are able to engage with materials flexibly and at their own pace • Students come to sessions with a required level of knowledge and understanding • Allows tutors to repurpose time for more engaging teaching approaches	• In-class tests • Peer-reviewed presentation • Practical activities(formative)	• Blackboard Collaborate • Blackboard discussion forums • Blackboard tests • Electronic Voting Systems • Podcasts • Resource lists online • Video
	Resource-centred or facilitated discussion *Tutors present artefacts and the class undertake self-directed discussion about them. Students might also select the artefact*	• Encourages expression of feelings, values, opinions and beliefs, and sharing of experiences • Presentation skills may be practised, building confidence and the ability for self-expression • Develops critical evaluation skills	• Demonstrations • Observation • Peer-review • Report	• Audio • Blackboard Collaborate • Blackboard discussion forums • Photos • Resource lists online • Skype • Video
	Micro-research *Students given a unique topic to research and later share their findings with the class*	• Development of presentation and/or other communication skills • Used for group work it can develop collaboration skills, but can also develop autonomy, independence and responsibility • Students can develop the learning materials for each other (potentially reusing them in subsequent cohorts)	• Infographic • Pecha Kucha • Poster • Presentation • Report • Student conference	• Audio • Presentation tools • Resource lists online • Video • Wikis

Figure 3.1   Teaching Approaches Menu

teaching, and students found them stimulating. However, this attitude from students quickly changed when every lecture had two or three polls in it. What appears novel and engaging can quickly become stale and annoying if it is used too much.

Tool types

Nerantzi and Beckingham's (2015) '5C Framework' provides a useful way to categorise tools based upon the student activity that they can support, namely Connecting; Communicating; Curating; Collaborating; and Creating. In this section, we will present examples of tools under these categories, though some tools are suitable for multiple categories. While this Framework centres on student activity, the same tools can also be used by teachers directly or while acting as facilitators. The following sections include specific examples of tools and technologies available at the time of writing, but, as technology evolves rapidly, it may be the case that these are no longer available or have been superseded by the time you read this. If this is the case, the broad categories should still be useful in finding more up-to-date alternatives.

Connecting

This category relates to activities and environments intended to enable students to build a community and develop relationships between individuals, ultimately leading to a robust and diverse learning network.

Social media
There can be few people who are unaware of social media, even if they do not use any themselves. While mostly used purely for social purposes, they can also bring significant benefits to teaching, particularly by allowing authentic outside voices and opinions to be brought into the classroom where they can be analysed, dissected and contrasted. This is particularly useful for making connections with outside experts but can also be used to show the 'real-world' implications of theory being explored by the students. The most commonly used social media tools worldwide, security and privacy issues notwithstanding, are Twitter, Facebook and WhatsApp; however, some tools are more popular in some parts of the world and with particular demographics, such as WeChat and Weibo in China and with Chinese students overseas due to the 'Western' tools being banned.

Professional presence
In addition to the more informal social media tools above there are tools that are particularly well suited for students to both develop a professional

presence and to make connections with professionals already working in the fields to which they aspire. Some, such as LinkedIn, are designed specifically for this purpose but others have grown organically to occupy this niche in addition to their more general use. A good example of the latter would be Instagram which, while commonly used for sharing images of users' lifestyles (or the lifestyles they want others to think they have!), has become a very popular place for professionals involved in the visual arts to showcase their work – especially important in an industry with a large number of freelancers.

Communicating

This category relates to tools that enable students to make use of the learning network to share ideas and experience, as well as question peers and teachers and provide their own responses to the questions of others.

Discussion board

A discussion board is a tool that enables teachers and students to ask and answer questions, as well as take part in longer debates prompted. Since they are usually used asynchronously, they allow students to conduct research and give more detailed, referenced responses than the rapid answers demanded by a synchronous tool. This makes them a good tool for boosting inclusivity. They can also be used for critiquing visual work, with students posting their work and the related discussion being critiqued by the other students. While public and commercial discussion board tools exist, they are a standard tool in institutional virtual learning environments (VLEs) and as such have inbuilt privacy and security.

Video conferencing/webinar

While the obvious use for this type of tool is to provide synchronous teaching sessions that replicate lectures, workshops and tutorials online, they can also be used for peer-to-peer communications between students. Much like social media tools, a significant opportunity provided by these tools is the ability to bring in outside voices from anywhere in the world. For example, with careful planning they can enable occupational health students to interview real service users; or civil engineering students to quiz practising engineers about a dam-building project. Examples of these tools include Zoom, Skype and Google Meet, all of which quickly gained popularity during the worldwide Covid-19 lockdown in 2020, but education-specific tools, such as Blackboard Collaborate and Adobe Connect are also widely used and integrate with institutional virtual learning environments. Free, open source video conferencing is also available with BigBlueButton and Jitsi.

Curating

This refers to tools to support students in independently finding, assessing and collating information that supports their learning. While curating is generally an individual activity, it can also incorporate others.

Personal curation
Organising materials, both self-created like meeting or session notes and external sources, is an important way of making sense of a large body of information, especially with complex, interconnected pieces of information. Tools such as Microsoft OneNote and Evernote allow individuals to gather and categorise information privately but can also be used for sharing these materials with others.

Social curation
In contrast to personal curation tools, these tools are primarily intended for their contents to be published. This does not necessarily mean that these tools are designed to be used collaboratively with multiple people collaborating, just that the curated material is not solely for private use. Possibly the most well-known social curation tool is Pinterest, which is used to collate web-based resources in a visual way, while Diigo is a tool that offers a more textual and list-based approach.

Academic resource curation
Tools such as Mendeley and Zotero are specialist tools with a very specific purpose: collating research outputs, categorising them and adding notes, and exporting subsets as reference lists for papers and reports. The main use of these tools is personal, but they can also be used collaboratively – something that is extremely useful for generating annotated bibliographies for group assessment.

Collaborating

Here we have tools that are used by students to explicitly work with others in sense-making activities, and collectively work on exploring problems or in producing shared outputs.

Collaborative document creation
Group activities and assessments are extremely common and they frequently incorporate the production of documents and presentations, but sharing these files and keeping track of changes by multiple people is often a challenge for students, while identifying the contribution of individuals is difficult for teachers when files are just emailed around and then submitted online.

Collaborative platforms such as Google Drive and Microsoft 365 provide online word processors, spreadsheets, presentation tools, file sharing and other tools that allow several people to make edits simultaneously while also tracking all changes, including details about the editor and when the edit was made. These tools can also be used by teachers to co-create materials with colleagues and students.

Project communication

An area of group work that students often struggle with is the coordination and tracking of activity. As this is also an issue in the workplace, particularly during enforced remote working due to Covid-19, tools are available to aid in communication and coordination among project teams. These tools generally provide ways for team members to share resources, mark progress and communicate with each other both synchronously and asynchronously. Two tools that have become very popular in the workplace, and increasingly so in higher education, are Slack and Microsoft Teams.

Voting/polling

Polling tools are a useful way to check understanding during a session, whether online or face to face. Video conferencing tools such as Zoom and Blackboard Collaborate frequently have polling features built in, making it very easy to question students. These could be related to the factual session content, or they could be to ask students their opinions about specific scenarios such as the best way to solve a given problem, thus creating a stimulus for discussion. Dedicated polling tools like Mentimeter and Kahoot can also be used for this purpose but have the advantage that they offer a wide range of question types and can present results in more varied ways, such as word clouds.

Creating

This final category relates to activities where students produce their own content in a creative way. The tools presented here vary significantly in their ease of use and should be investigated and simpler alternatives selected where required.

Media

One way for both teachers and students to show their creativity and produce engaging materials is through creating media outputs, such as images, audio and video. Regardless of the type of material that you or your students want to produce there will likely be an online tool that makes it easy to achieve, often for free. Engaging animated videos can be created with tools such as Powtoon, while video presentations can be produced with Adobe Spark. Screencast-o-matic is well suited for recording more traditional presentations, along with demonstrations of software, walk-throughs of web pages and other situations where capturing the screen is required. Tools such as Canva can be used to create attractive posters and infographics, while Microsoft Sway can be used for making engaging presentations and newsletters.

Blogs

Due to their diary-like, time-based nature, blogs are extremely well suited to use by students for documenting long-term processes and projects, both for personal reflection and as a formal part of assessment. Commercial tools such as WordPress and Blogger have the potential advantage that the work can be made available publicly and so serve as a showcase for the student, while the blog tools contained within most virtual learning environments have the opposite advantage that they preserve the privacy of the student and ensure that their work and ideas are not shared publicly.

Showcasing/portfolio

While blogs can be an effective way for students to create and share show-cases of their work, there are other tools that are either designed for this purpose or otherwise well suited to it. PebblePad gives individuals a significant amount of control and customisation when it comes to creating portfolios and showcases because, in common with other tools like Google Sites, students can structure their content in whatever way suits their purpose, incorporating images, video and audio as well as text and documents. There are also many other tools that are de-facto showcases for students and professionals, such as Instagram. For computing students, in particular, GitHub is a place to showcase coding projects. Having a public presence is becoming increasingly expected in certain professions so it is worth encouraging your students to explore what platforms are popular within their discipline.

Case study

Background

Sandra is a Course Leader for a Software Engineering course as well as being departmental Employability Lead. She was concerned that, while students were learning the core skills and knowledge on the course, they were not getting some of the less technical, but highly sought-after, skills needed for working as a programmer. From her contacts in industry it was apparent that large parts of the industry were moving towards projects using virtual teams who were often spread across different countries.

Teaching on the course was heavily focused on the individual acquisition of technical skills, such as a variety of programming languages and design methodologies, but included some group projects.

Change

Sandra wanted the students to develop the skills and knowledge that would allow them to work confidently in virtual teams. Amending the assessment designs in several modules to group projects, she organised access to the relevant industry-standard tools, including Slack and Microsoft Teams for project communications, Trello for task management and coordination, and a private GitHub for managing code and other project outputs. She then ensured that the students were introduced to these technologies and had a chance to gain experience in their use with some early formative activities. Finally, she arranged weekly project meetings with the student groups to emulate how things work in industry.

Outcome

Students returning from placements where this project approach was used stated that the opportunity to experience it during their studies gave them a significant confidence boost during their placement and allowed them to settle into this way of working much quicker than would otherwise have been the case. They also felt that they had gained valuable skills that would help them in the job market. Sandra has also heard from her contacts that the students from her course are generally able to begin contributing to projects sooner than other students because they already have an understanding of the necessary tools, processes and etiquette.

REFLECTIVE ACTIVITY 3.1

- Find out which online learning tools are supported by your institution (you may be able to get this information from the relevant team at your institution).
- List the pros and cons of using each of these within your context.
- What combination of tools will best work for your course/module?

Having introduced a range of tools for supporting or enabling effective online learning, in the following chapter we look at ways in which to design them into courses, modules and individual sessions.

Further reading

Kathy Schrock's Online Tools Guide, https://www.schrockguide.net/online-tools. html (accessed 5 September 2020).

A regularly updated list of online tools categorised by purpose for online learning.

2020 EDUCAUSE Horizon Report: Teaching and Learning Edition, https://www. educause.edu/horizon-report-2020 (accessed 5 September 2020).

The latest edition (at the time of writing) of EDUCAUSE's annual report on trends and the future of technology in education.

References

Beetham, H. and Sharpe, S. (2007) An introduction to rethinking pedagogy for a digital age. In Beetham and Sharpe (eds), *Rethinking Pedagogy for a Digital Age: Designing and Delivering E-Learning*, 1–10. London: Taylor and Francis.

Glover, I., Hepplestone, S., Parkin, H., Rodger, H. and Irwin, B. (2016) Pedagogy first: realising technology enhanced learning by focusing on teaching practice. *British Journal of Educational Technology*, 47(5), 993–1002.

Kirkwood, A. (2015) Teaching and learning with technology in higher education: blended and distance education needs 'joined-up thinking' rather than technological determinism. *Open Learning*, 29(3), 206–21.

Nerantzi, C. and Beckingham, S. (2015) BYOD4L: Learning to use own smart devices for learning and teaching through the 5C framework. In Middleton, A. (ed.), *Smart Learning: Teaching and Learning with Smartphones and Tablets in Post-Compulsory Education*. Sheffield: MELSIG.

Rogers, E. (2003) *Diffusion of Innovations* (5th edn). London: Simon and Schuster.

Sheffield Hallam University (2014) *Teaching Approaches Menu*. Available online at: https://go.shu.ac.uk/teachingapproachesmenu (accessed 16 September 2020).

4

STRUCTURING ONLINE LEARNING

CHAPTER SUMMARY

This chapter starts with a look at how courses are often structured before looking at some of the ways in which a move to online learning can change this. We introduce a mnemonic to help think about different elements that inform or are influenced by a course structure and then highlight some of the wider aspects that affect the learning experience and are often implicit in face-to-face learning but need to be explicitly considered in online learning. We conclude with a case study that shows how an online learning experience was conceived and implemented, along with the impact on learners.

Introduction

Now that we've looked at the need to make our learning environment as inclusive as possible for our learners (Chapter 2) and identified some of the tools that we can use to provide that environment (Chapter 3) we can start to think about how to structure the learning experience. Traditionally, higher education has followed a formal structure based around large-scale information transmission, such as through a lecture, followed by opportunities for smaller groups of learners to explore, contextualise and apply that information, often through tutorials, seminars, workshops and labs. While a similar 'information→application' approach can be a valid structure in online learning, the nature of online learning and its ready access to multiple sources of information, opportunities for interaction between peers and with outside experts, and myriad ways for learners to build and present their developing understanding offers alternative structures and designs that can help empower learners to take greater control of their learning.

Opportunities provided by online learning

The traditional course structure of higher education largely places the teacher at the centre. It is they who define the content that is taught, the sequence in which it is taught and the methods by which it is taught. They select the specific knowledge and skills that are to be assessed and the standard to which the learners are to be compared. This teacher-centric approach is comparable to a car assembly line where the cars (the learners) travel a common path along which they are gradually constructed, with new parts (knowledge) being added in sequence until they roll off the end a completed vehicle (graduate). In both the car and graduate assembly lines there are some opportunities for differentiation, such as adding a different engine or paint colour for the car or allowing the choice of a few topics to study during the course and working on a personally selected dissertation/project for the learner, but the process results in outputs that are very similar. Online learning can change this completely.

Online learning has the potential to change the learning experience on several levels: session ('micro' level); module ('meso' level); and course ('macro' level). These levels (Figure 4.1) are related but have some independence from each other in that changes at any level may not require changes in others, though it is more likely that changes at higher levels will require changes to those below.

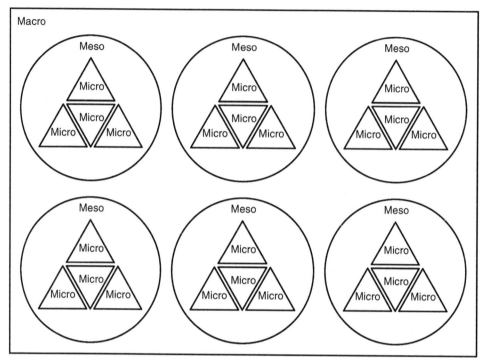

Figure 4.1   Relationship between macro, meso and micro levels

Micro

It is the micro level where the changes brought about by the move to online learning are most obvious. The fact that the learners don't come together in a shared physical space means that online learning looks and feels different, yet it is still possible to follow the traditional 'information→application' structure, as was seen during the rapid switch to online learning as a result of worldwide lockdowns due to the Covid-19 pandemic in 2020 (Watermeyer *et al.*, 2020). The speed at which learning moved online meant that there was little time to consider alternative ways to teach in many cases, and this may have led to the worst of both worlds: a didactic teaching approach coupled with physically and mentally isolated learners.

However, the sophistication and ready availability of a wide range of communication and creative tools means that alternative, effective learning activities are more possible than ever before. Many teachers make full use of the fact that the tools used to take part in online learning are the same as those required for a wide range of other activities, such as producing materials to be submitted for assessment or future professional practice (Luo *et al.*, 2017). For example, by maximising the value of synchronous contact time by pre-recording information delivery for learners to watch before sessions using the same tools that learners would use to create their own recorded presentations, or encouraging peer learning and the incorporation of different viewpoints, opinions and experiences through social media.

Meso

Many university lecturers find themselves operating at this level, having been given a module to 'lead' on an established programme of study, often with a predetermined scheme of work, mapping out what is to be 'covered' each week. Teaching a module online affords the opportunity to think in a less linear way, so instead of adopting a session-by-session 'information→ application' model, we are freed up to envisage alternative ways of learning and the structures that enable them.

An example is given in Table 4.1 and Figure 4.2 below.

Table 4.1   Research methods module scheme of work (traditional), face-to-face linear approach

Week	Topic (Lecture)	Topic (Seminar)
1	Introduction to research and ethics	Reading and discussing example research reports
2	Writing your research question	Discussing researchable topics and writing RQs
3	Writing your literature review	Reading and discussing example literature reviews
4	Choosing your overall methodology and selecting your research methods	Applying content on methodology/ methods to own research project
5	Approaches to data analysis	Attempting to analyse some sample data
6	Pulling it all together – discussing findings and drawing conclusions	Looking at sample research texts and how they approach the final sections

Approaches such as the one outlined in Figure 4.2 require careful planning and coordination. There is still a degree of linearity in that synchronous sessions need to be timetabled and put in a certain order, but there is also an emphasis on the learners finding things out for themselves and creating and uploading their own contributions, and a sense of knowledge being constructed by the community, with input from professionals in the field.

Mistakes I made when starting out

5-minute 'tell all' videos from early career researchers confessing their worst errors (ethical, methodological, etc.). Students watch these in their own time and write down any questions they have.

Live panel discussion with same researchers answering questions from students, who collaboratively compile a set of top tips for when they embark on their own research.

What am I going to research?

Small group discussions and meetings with supervisor to identify research topic and write questions.

Analysing sample research texts

Students work in groups online and look at an example research report. Each group has a different section (rationale, lit.review, methods, ethics, etc.) to answer questions on (What's this section about? What's in it? What purpose does it serve and how does it fit with the rest of the report? What points is the writer trying to make, and how do they go about it? Make a checklist of things to include in this section. Be prepared to present your results to the others).

How am I going to research it?

Video on pros and cons of different methods. Students have to watch this in their own time and then choose their own research approach and write a rationale for their choice, posting it on a discussion forum for feedback from a wider audience (course team, peers, other researchers).

Why my research matters

Students have their own '3-minute thesis' competition, making short videos about their projects. Experts from industry are invited to judge the results.

Who gets harmed and how can I prevent it?

Students discuss case studies of research projects with ethical issues, and then assess each other's project proposals from an ethical perspective.

Figure 4.2   A non-linear approach to an online research methods module

Other potential structures for modules include:

- a series of synchronous taught sessions with wraparound pre- and post-session asynchronous activities;
- a series of individual and group asynchronous activities, supported by 'how to' videos with technical content and drop-in online workshops and tutorial sessions;
- a work-based research project where students carry out individual desk-based and field research, with supervisory meetings online and occasional group seminars;
- a curated collection of resources that provide starting points for students to autonomously explore a topic at will, with the aim of producing an artefact for assessment. Online support from the teacher is provided according to the learner's instigation rather than as a regular, formal activity.

Macro

During the 2010s, there was significant interest (and hype) focused on the way that the internet could disrupt the prevailing model of higher education, in both a pedagogical and a business sense. This was centred on the concept of the massive open online course (MOOC) and how it might allow learners to create their own programmes of study based on their personal needs and interests, sequencing their own learning and studying across multiple institutions – and all for free (Pappano, 2012)! A central aspect of MOOCs is scale, with potentially tens of thousands of learners all studying the course at the same time. This means that there is necessarily a shift in focus away from the teacher as the source of knowledge towards individuals and peer communities finding, creating and sharing information.

While the original hype around MOOCs has reduced and commercialisation has taken place, they have shown that it is possible to allow learners to build their own personal curricula from a wide selection of topics and, more than that, they have shown that a greater emphasis on community and interaction can still help learners to meet both their own and the course learning objectives. While this level of flexibility is unlikely to be attainable in formal programmes of study, it does raise the question of whether the orthodox approach of a single sequence of modules, some of which are prerequisites for others, is the most effective way to structure learning. Online learning may offer a way for learners to sequence their learning in ways that work better for their existing understanding and ambitions, such as by swapping some notionally 'second year' modules for some 'first year' ones, by removing some of the influence of the need to timetable physical spaces and prevent clashes so that learners can take modules entirely asynchronously if necessary. Such an approach would reinforce the move away from teacher-centred learning towards learners being more in control of their own studies.

REFLECTIVE ACTIVITY 4.1

How are your courses currently structured at the macro, meso and micro levels?

What changes might online learning allow you to make? What do you definitely need to retain?

Be an online learning barista

Designing and structuring online learning is a bit like being a coffee barista. For the uninitiated it can look straightforward, yet it requires a surprising level of technical skill, theoretical understanding, deftness and creativity developed with time and experience. As a guide to this process, we present the ingredients of the LATTE (Learning units, Activities, Timing, Tools and Environment).

Learning units

By potentially breaking the traditional learning structure that is in large part the result of constraints due to the need to efficiently use physical spaces, online learning provides new ways to structure the module. Sessions need not be designed around hour-long blocks and can be adapted to the needs of the material being covered, particularly for asynchronous activities. Existing lectures can be broken into smaller pieces that focus on a single idea, theory, concept, or skill, with exercises and activities that encourage the learners to integrate the new knowledge into their existing understanding. This results in learning units that are then combined to meet the desired overall learning objectives for the module or course. This process can be seen to an extent in the example shown above in Figure 4.2.

Activities

Online learning supports a wide range of learning activities, from online equivalents of traditional activities such as discussions and reflective writing through to ones that are only possible due to the underlying technology such as creating an animated video or exploring historical sites through 360 degree photos and video. Even in situations where the activity itself is little different, there may be ways to use the technology to enhance the experience – perhaps by using reflective videos as an option instead of writing or by 'publishing' the results of the activities on appropriate social media platforms.

Puentedura's (2012) 'Substitution–Augmentation–Modification–Redefinition' (SAMR) model offers a way to consider how existing learning activities can be changed as a result of incorporating technology. The lowest levels, Substitution and Augmentation, show the least difference between pre- and post-technology introduction and are classed as 'Enhancement', while the higher levels, Modification and Redefinition, use the available technology to dramatically alter the activity and are classed as 'transformation'. While SAMR is not without its own limitations, including the potential for pedagogy to be led by technology and generally encouraging users of the model to work within their existing knowledge rather than seeking out new approaches (Bauder *et al.*, 2019), it can be useful when reviewing alternative ideas for activities.

Timing

As part of the planning around learning units and activities it is important to consider the timing of these. By this we mean both the sequencing of units and activities such that the learners are able to gradually develop their knowledge in a logical manner (for example, by making sure that later sessions and activities build on earlier ones) and whether synchronous or asynchronous is the most appropriate approach. For example, it is generally best to maximise the learning value of the limited 'live' (synchronous) situations available during a module, therefore content-heavy teaching methods such as lectures are likely to be better being delivered asynchronously, such as through recording the delivery of the material, meaning that the synchronous session can focus on interaction. The literal timing of 'live' sessions is also something to consider, particularly where your learners are in different time zones or where they are likely to have work and family commitments that make attending timetabled sessions difficult.

Synchronous vs asynchronous

There are advantages to both synchronous and asynchronous approaches to teaching. For example, the immediacy of synchronous methods can help build strong interpersonal connections and be more responsive to learners' needs and existing understanding, while asynchronous methods can encourage deeper engagement by giving learners a longer period over which to think, research and reflect before making a contribution. In terms of deciding whether to run a session or a series of activities synchronously or asynchronously, the flowchart in Figure 4.3 may be of some help. Note that you may need to break down a session that was previously taught face to face into smaller learning units and evaluate each of them individually in order to decide whether they should be taught synchronously or asynchronously.

So, for example, if, on the one hand, your planned synchronous session is in the form of a traditional lecture, with no opportunities for interaction from the audience, you may as well create a video (or a series of short videos or related activities – see Chapter 5) and let the students access this asynchronously (in their own time). If, on the other hand, you would like students to be able to compare and discuss their approaches to solving problems set the week before, or to be on hand yourself to answer questions, then a synchronous session may be more appropriate (see Chapter 6).

Tools

The tools that we looked at in Chapter 3 were centred around those that are likely to be formally provided by the institution. Selecting the appropriate tool for the desired learning experience is important and will be a factor of the type of activity and the timing. However, it is important to remember that learners will have personal preferences around which tools they want to use and may have a variety of reasons for their choice. While there might be opportunities to allow individuals or small groups to select their own

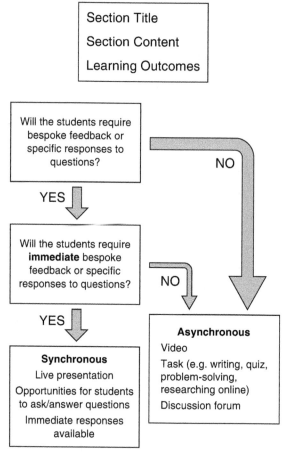

Figure 4.3   Deciding when to teach synchronously online and when to teach asynchronously online

tools from a range of appropriate options, particularly when related to creative activities and assessments, it may be necessary to 'force' learners to use tools contrary to their personal preference. In these situations, it is useful to have a sound justification for your choice to prevent it appearing as an arbitrary or purely personal choice. Examples of justifications may be security of personal data; tool provided and managed by the institution; cost; use in industry; comparability; and, most importantly, pedagogical alignment.

As an example, you may want learners to create a portfolio of reflections on their learning over the course. You could give learners the freedom to select whatever tool they feel would work best for their own skills and interest, and receive a mix of portfolios of video reflections, of drawings, or of text. This may not be a problem if the assessment criteria are fully abstracted away from the format, but it would cause problems if part of the assessment is explicitly of the learner's reflective writing skills. In this case, you may provide a list of acceptable tools, such as the blogging tools within the virtual learning environment or external tools like WordPress, Blogger or Google Sites. This would still give the learners an opportunity to select a tool but would also enable you to ensure that the core requirements of the assessment can be met.

Environment

As we saw in Chapter 2 when looking at accessibility and inclusive practices, the environment in which the activities take place and the tools used exist is an important consideration. The online environment provides a range of information sources, alternative perspectives and other people to interact with and learn from. While this can seem undesirable to teachers who have carefully planned and coordinated the learners' experience, it is actually extremely valuable and learners should be encouraged to look beyond the sources provided by the teacher as this will help them develop learning autonomy. In this sense, a large part of what the teacher does in an online environment is facilitate the learner to explore and construct new understanding for themselves, so rather than fearing this loss of control we should embrace the new opportunities that the online environment brings.

However, learners can sometimes find online environments loaded with lots of different resources quite intimidating. It's therefore essential to structure the resource logically and to make it clear what is essential, core reading or viewing, what is there as further general background knowledge and what is there as optional extras, perhaps looking at particular topics in more depth. The virtual learning environment can often assist with this by allowing teachers to set formative tests and release particular materials based on performance, so that learners who do extremely well will be directed to more advanced, optional materials while those who struggled would be directed to simpler materials that will help clarify the fundamental concepts. This level of differentiation is useful for maintaining interest and engagement in learners regardless of their level of understanding without overwhelming them with information that is unsuitable for their level of understanding.

Learners should also be encouraged to keep a learning log or build a portfolio of their online activity, or else report back on their reading and research. This helps to keep them engaged and serves to provide different models of the learning process between peers.

The teacher's role here is to help the learners make sense of what they are finding out and to enable them to see how things fit together to make a bigger picture. They need to be supported in selecting relevant content and discarding other content, in critiquing what they find and in making links to the module learning outcomes and assessment tasks. Regular synchronous plenaries can help with this process and maintain a sense of being part of a larger group.

REFLECTIVE ACTIVITY 4.2

Think about the current LATTE 'recipe' for your course. How can you adapt it to online delivery so that it meets the requirements of both the learners and the overall course?

Thinking holistically

While we have been considering the structure of the learning experience at a number of different levels, there are also a range of other elements that contribute to the overall experience, such as the development of a learning community and learner wellbeing. These elements are often considered as either secondary to, or emergent from, the choices made regarding content, activities, assessments and curriculum. In some ways the need to explicitly consider these aspects of the overall learning experience is more important for online learning than in traditional face-to-face learning. While the promotion and provision of them on campus is likely to be the responsibility of someone other than the teacher, online the teacher may need to at least make learners aware of their existence and, in some cases, actually provide them directly. For example, some teaching staff may find that their tutorials become dominated by learners' financial or mental health concerns since, being off campus, the learner feels unable to access the appropriate services. It is important, therefore, that teachers are familiar with the support services being provided by the university and how these might be operating at a remote level.

A major aspect of the learning experience that needs to be deliberately nurtured in an online setting is that of course community. On campus, learners are likely to spend time with each other between teaching sessions because they are moving between physical spaces together, but online even a short gap between sessions is likely to mean that learners will log off and do something individually rather than stay online with each other. Therefore, it is important to incorporate activities into sessions that encourage learners to get to know each other, from ice-breakers in early sessions to regular group work across the course to dedicating the last few minutes of synchronous sessions to an opportunity for learners to chat about other things.

While building a course community will help, learners may still feel isolated when learning online. It can be more difficult for teachers to identify learners who may be struggling when compared to on-campus teaching because it is more difficult to pick up non-verbal cues about how they are feeling when using online tools, even synchronous ones. So, the need for pastoral activities that help support wellbeing and inclusion is high. While these may already be a formal part of the course, providing additional opportunities and signposting existing support and services will greatly benefit learners. Offering open 'office hours' where learners are able to speak with you, whether through online tools or over the phone, is advisable as a way to supplement more formal arrangements while also helping to manage your own time more effectively.

Formal mentoring, from learners further along in the course or alumni, and less formal peer-supported learning groups can also be an excellent way of building course community, inspiring individual learners and boosting inclusivity by explicitly valuing diversity. These could be online activities, but there may also be opportunities for learners to form their own face-to-face study groups should there be enough of them in a given location. This 'organic' face-to-face peer learning element has proven successful in motivating learners in MOOCs and in helping build course community (Chen and Chen, 2015). Mentoring is a different approach and one that will likely require more management by the teacher but can prove to be a very valuable experience for both the mentor and the mentee.

REFLECTIVE ACTIVITY 4.3

What techniques do you use and what opportunities do you provide to support the learner's experience holistically in face-to-face teaching? How would you translate these to online teaching?

What is missing? How could you incorporate these into the teaching and wider course experience in an online programme?

Case study

David is a Radiotherapy lecturer and wanted to create a short, open, free course that would explore issues around prostate cancer and be suitable for a mixed cohort of medical practitioners, patients, survivors, family members and members of the public. The course needed to be quite short in order to appeal to people with a range of external commitments, and the wide variety of knowledge and experience within the intended audience meant that the materials provided needed to be both informative for people with a medical background, yet accessible to lay people. In addition, the course was intended as a way for practitioners to learn from the experience of patients and their families while enabling the lay people to gain a deeper insight into prostate cancer care and treatment by interacting with medical professionals.

Working with academic colleagues, learning technology specialists and external contacts, including the Prostate Cancer UK charity, David designed the course around four themes, with the learning and activities for each taking place over the course of a week, along with an initial 'induction' week to help develop the required technical skills to take part in the course. The course was hosted using the PebblePad portfolio and personal learning tool, with a digital workbook being provided for each theme that contained materials along with exercises for the participants to complete. Each week followed a regular pattern of roughly hour-long activities, with the new material released on Monday, a reflective activity on Tuesday, a live Twitter discussion on Wednesday, a private small group discussion that deliberately mixed professionals and lay people on Thursday and reflective writing on Friday – though the learners could do the asynchronous activities at other times. If participants submitted their reflective writing, they would have it commented upon by the academics and be issued with a digital badge to share on social media and reflect their participation that week. For medical professionals, collecting all of the badges and submitting them with a further reflection would allow them to claim equivalent credit to completing a module if applying for a relevant Master's degree at the university, saving them time and money if choosing to pursue further study.

The MOOC was successful, ran several times and had hundreds of regularly engaged participants from around the world. It resulted in significant advances being made in this area (Obu, 2015). The structure of the course met the aims of providing a valuable learning experience for both professionals and lay people, through combining formal teaching and academic materials with community and peer activity.

Closing thoughts

In this chapter we have looked at the three levels of the learning experience and how these can be used to guide the design of online learning. The LATTE mnemonic offers a structured way to think about online learning design and helps to encourage a holistic view that considers the importance of how both the learning design and the wider context in which the learning takes place can affect the learning experience. By considering the different levels and thinking holistically, we can design online learning that is engaging, effective and exciting.

Further reading

Benson, R. and Brack, C. (2010) *Online Learning and Assessment in Higher Education: A Planning Guide*. Oxford/Cambridge/New Delhi: Chandos. Chapter 3: Online learning design and development, 55–106.

In the fast-moving world of technology this chapter may seem a little dated in some ways, but in fact it has much relevance for the current context. Beginning with theoretical approaches to planning and design, it moves on to practical ideas and advice involving a range of activities.

Kranzow, J. (2013) Faculty leadership in online education: structuring courses to impact student satisfaction and persistence. *Journal of Online Learning and Teaching*, 9(1), 131–9.

A short article focusing on the more holistic aspects of online course design, such as motivation and community.

Major, C. (2015) *Teaching Online: A Guide to Theory, Research, and Practice*. Baltimore: Johns Hopkins University Press. Chapter 5: Course planning, 109–30.

A clear and practical guide to planning online learning, interspersed with detailed case studies.

Raisinghani, M.S. (ed.) (2013) *Curriculum, Learning, and Teaching Advancements in Online Education*. Pennsylvania: IGI Global.

International case studies of different approaches to online learning, using a range of tools and approaches.

References

Bauder, D.K., Cooper, K.M. and Simmons, T.J. (2019) SAMR strategies for the integration of technology through UDL. *Universal Access Through Inclusive Instructional Design: International Perspectives on UDL*, 141.

Chen, Y.-H. and Chen, P-J. (2015) MOOC study group: facilitation strategies, influential factors, and student perceived gains. *Computers and Education*, 86, 55–0. https://doi.org/10.1016/j.compedu.2015.03.008

Luo, T., Murray, A. and Crompton, H. (2017) Designing authentic learning activities to train pre-service teachers about teaching online. *International Review of Research in Open and Distributed Learning*, 18(7). https://doi.org/10.19173/irrodl.v18i7.3037

Obu, R.N. (2015) *Case study: Impact of the Enhancing Prostate Cancer MOOC*. Available online at: https://www.academia.edu/15290352/Case_Study_Impact_of_the_enhancing_Prostate_Cancer_MOOC (accessed 31 October 2020).

Pappano, L. (2012) The year of the MOOC. *The New York Times*, 2 November. Available online at: http://www.nytimes.com/2012/11/04/education/edlife/massive-open-online-courses-are-multiplying-at-a-rapid-pace.html?_r=0 (accessed 4 November 2020).

Puentedura, R.R. (2012) *Building upon SAMR*. Presentation slides. Available online at: http://hippasus.com/rrpweblog/archives/2012/09/03/BuildingUponSAMR.pdf (accessed 2 October 2020).

Watermeyer, R., Crick, T., Knight, C. and Goodall, J. (2020) COVID-19 and digital disruption in UK universities: afflictions and affordances of emergency online migration. *Higher Education*. Available online at: https://doi.org/10.1007/s10734-020-00561-y (accessed 2 October 2020).

5

PRESENTING ONLINE

CHAPTER SUMMARY

In this chapter we look at how to move from a traditional 'on-campus' lecture to a set of interactive online learning experiences. The focus here is on *asynchronous* learning – in particular, the recording of lectures, as well as other ways of presenting knowledge in an online environment. Facilitating *synchronous* learning is discussed in Chapter 6 and we explore more activity-based *asynchronous* learning in Chapter 7.

Transferring lecture content to an online environment requires more than uploading one's slides or filming a face-to-face lecture. After looking at video presentation skills, we suggest some creative alternatives to the traditional lecture. We then present a case study set of lecture slides that can be converted into a series of online-friendly formats.

'I know kung fu'

In the sci-fi film *The Matrix*, the character Neo is taught the art of kung fu by being plugged into a computer and having the knowledge and skills quite literally downloaded into his brain. In fact, the traditional university lecture is designed on much the same principle. In a lecture, the focus is on talking for the purpose of educating the audience, and the assumption is that knowledge is 'transmitted' by the lecturer and 'received' by the learner. In practice, however, the process is not quite that simple. Sadly (some would say), students do not simply 'download' the knowledge that is presented to them and emerge from the lecture theatre as mini versions of the lecturer. From a constructivist perspective, for learning to take place the students must process the new knowledge that is presented to them, shaping and aligning it according to prior experiences, deconstructing earlier misconceptions and reconstructing their perceived realities (von Glasersfeld, 1995).

If this is the case, then teaching should be designed to create opportunities for learners to engage actively with what is being taught (see, for example, Allen and Baughman, 2016). In a face-to-face lecture, there are many opportunities for spontaneous interaction – questions and answers, short tasks, asking students to vote on a range of possible solutions, discussions and so on. To an extent the same is true in synchronous online teaching. In a pre-recorded 'lecture', however, the challenge of creating such interactions becomes seemingly impossible.

Terminology and contexts

In this chapter we will be replacing the term 'lecture' with that of 'presentation'. Here, we take 'presentation' to mean the introduction of knowledge in a format where instantaneous learner feedback is impossible, due to the pre-recorded or pre-designed nature of the presentation. In higher education, this can happen in different ways.

Examples of presentations in video format

- **An on-campus 'lecture' that has been captured** – that is, filmed and uploaded for students to access in their own time. This sometimes involves synchronising the lecturer's voice with the appropriate presentation slides, but it can also be created simply by filming the whole thing from the back of the room and uploading it to a VLE. This can be available in video format or via software that allows the viewer to annotate the content as they are watching (for example, Echo or Panopto). Lecture capture is popular with some students as it enables them to catch up on missed lectures or to review course content prior to an assessment (Khee *et al.*, 2014). In our experience, the videos are not necessarily watched linearly from start to finish – key parts may be played several times, other parts skipped over and sometimes the footage is played back at up to 1.5 times the original speed in order to save time! Perhaps a whole hour straight of a talking head with slides is simply too long to hold the viewer's attention any other way (Thomson *et al.*, 2014).

- **A pre-recorded video made by the tutor**, often in their own home, sometimes as a screen capture of a slide presentation with an audio commentary and sometimes as the presenter speaking directly into the camera. This often has a more informal feel than a lecture capture approach and it has been shown that students respond well to the sound of their own tutor's voice, *ums*, *ahs* and all. In practice, however, these videos are often too long.

- **An animated video made by the teacher** – for example, using *Powtoon* (powtoon.com/), involving graphics, audio commentary and often background music. The novelty value of an animated presentation has the potential to hold the viewer's attention and, if well designed, the visual images and movements can enhance the meaning of the content (for example, items in a list arriving on the screen one by one). The disadvantage of this approach is that it can be very time-consuming to create such a video, added to which there is a danger of causing cognitive and sensory overload, particularly if background music is used. This means that the 'less is more' principle should apply to the design; in other words, keep it simple. If a lot of animation is used – for example, using an app that provides templates of slides with moving images – students may like the novelty factor at first, but will quickly tire of anything too 'flashy' or 'gimmicky'. Any animation used should enhance and complement the meaning of the text or audio commentary, not distract from it.

- **A bespoke video made by a professional film crew** – for example, with multiple camera angles, locations, actors, props and further special effects. The results can be effective, but the cost is often prohibitive.

- **An 'off the shelf' video**, such as one produced by an educational publisher or one from a shared platform such as YouTube – for example, a TED talk (ted.com/talks). This has the advantage of being cheap and convenient. However, it can sometimes take time to find the 'right' video for the purpose of the session and the results can vary in quality.

- **A student-led presentation**, where the students design and facilitate the introduction of knowledge and present this to their peers. In an online environment, students can be asked to produce short videos. This can be quite time-consuming, and students can require a high level of support as they get to grips with the technology involved.

> **REFLECTIVE ACTIVITY 5.1**
>
> Watch a few minutes of a documentary film on a topic of your choosing. Note down the ways in which the film captures and sustains the viewer's attention and motivation to keep watching.

Thoughts

Documentary makers use many techniques to hold the viewer's attention – a range of camera angles, locations, background music and presenters, shots of people walking or engaging in activities, other actors (e.g. local experts), judicious editing, background music and even animations. In fact, the amount of effort that is expended to stop the viewer from switching off (literally and figuratively) is enormous. Unless you can afford to hire a professional film crew and have vast amounts of free time, however, these options are not likely to be available to you.

So, if all you have is a set of slides, one camera and your own self as the presenter, plus a limited amount of time in which to create your video, where do you begin?

There are some simple techniques that documentary makers use that can help you. Adding some intonation and expression to your voice is one, and having a clear structure and narrative to the presentation is another. Using visual stimuli also helps – for example, authentic and appropriate images that complement the text and reflect a diversity of contexts and people.

When creating an audio commentary, avoid simply reading out the text on the slides. This is something that a screen-reader app will do, for those students who need it. Instead, enhance the points on the slide by adding, for example, some critical analysis, stories from the sector (including global perspectives), or by citing supporting research or theory. Try to be human – stumbling over your words or coughing occasionally is acceptable and creates spontaneity. Try not to read from a script as you are likely to sound unnatural and stilted. Use humour – introduce your cat or grumble when you have to pause the recording because your phone is ringing. If your face is visible, make sure you look at the camera as you speak (Thomson *et al.*, 2014). You will also need to consider how to make your speech accessible to someone who cannot access your audio output. Will you use captions or provide a transcript? Conversely, you may need to provide alternative text for outputs that are purely visual in nature (an image or an animation). Chapter 2 has more on inclusive design.

Another way to engage your viewers is to set short tasks and invite the student to stop the video at key points. You can then provide comments/answers in the following slide. Some lecture capture systems such as Echo or Panopto can even be used to make the video pause automatically at certain points.

Above all, keep videos short. As a very rough guide, a 'talking head' video should have a playback time of no more than three minutes; one with visual input such as slides, no more than around 10–15 minutes; and one with other features such as a variety of locations or presenters, no more than 20–25 minutes. Remember also that longer videos can be broken up into shorter 'chunks'.

Make the purpose of your video clear, with links to the wider module, course and assessment requirements and, where possible, the world of work. Explain how long the students can expect it to take, including any tasks or questions set where they might want to pause the recording. Finally, make it clear whether watching the video is a core or optional requirement, the date by which it needs to have been viewed and whether students' answers to the tasks in the video need to be shared with the tutor (for example, via a quiz app or posted to a discussion board).

Other ways of 'presenting'

It is worth noting that video is not the only medium through which you can present knowledge from a distance. Here are a few.

- **A 'self-access' set of presentation slides**, which the student works through in slideshow mode, reading the content as they go, sometimes with added audio commentary. Sometimes the slides are accompanied by an avatar representing the presenter.
- **A sound file or audio podcast**. The advantage of these is that students can listen to them while out and about or multi-tasking. The disadvantage is that communication is occurring via one sense only, which carries the danger of a loss in concentration from the listener.
- **A text** of some sort – for example, a journal article, a 'hand out', a book chapter or a webpage, sometimes presented in the form of a shared document on the Cloud, for students to annotate collaboratively and discuss. Commercial collaborative reading software is also available for this purpose.
- **An infographic**, perhaps with audio commentary. However, these can be time-consuming to prepare and may not be as accessible or as clear as you think.
- **A quiz** or task with feedback embedded into it, so that the student gets to 'have a go' and then look at a suggested solution or commentary.
- **A series of questions** for which the student must find the answers by doing their own research – for example, by looking up library sources or contacting 'experts' in the field.
- **A discussion forum** that students are instructed to contribute to, with the teacher facilitating the discussion and providing further input where needed in order to fill any gaps in knowledge.

Food and Mood
The impact of diet on mental health

MODULE: ISSUES IN NUTRITION
25TH JANUARY

What is depression?

How might diet be
linked to mood and
depression?

DISCUSS IN PAIRS FOR 2 MINUTES

Learning Outcomes for today

By the end of the session you will be able to:

1. Define depression
2. Describe the aetiology and symptoms of depression
3. Identify and explain how dietary factors might influence mood
4. Critically review some of the literature on this topic
5. Develop dietary strategies for a person with mild depression, and justify your approach

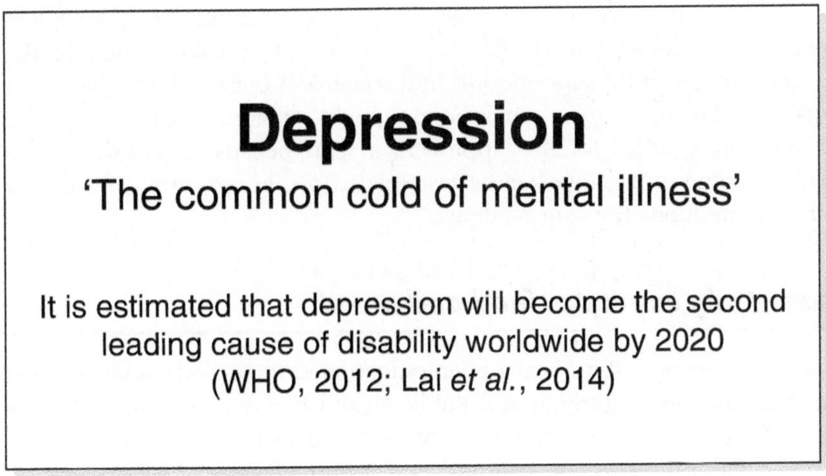

Depression
'The common cold of mental illness'

It is estimated that depression will become the second leading cause of disability worldwide by 2020 (WHO, 2012; Lai *et al.*, 2014)

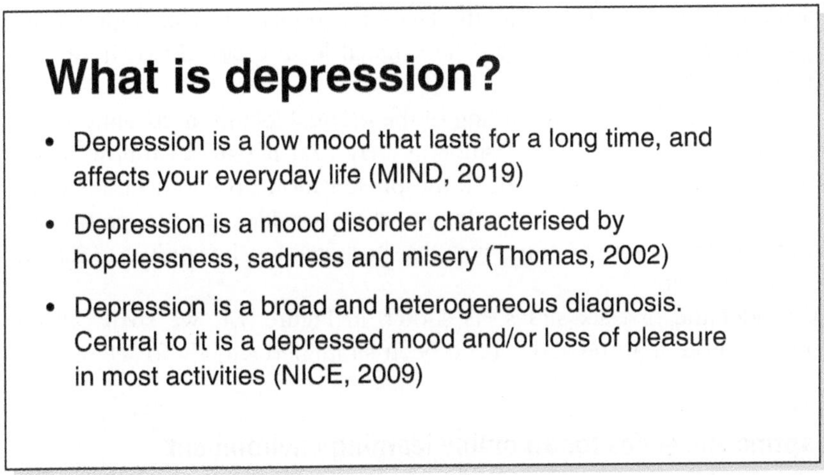

What is depression?

- Depression is a low mood that lasts for a long time, and affects your everyday life (MIND, 2019)

- Depression is a mood disorder characterised by hopelessness, sadness and misery (Thomas, 2002)

- Depression is a broad and heterogeneous diagnosis. Central to it is a depressed mood and/or loss of pleasure in most activities (NICE, 2009)

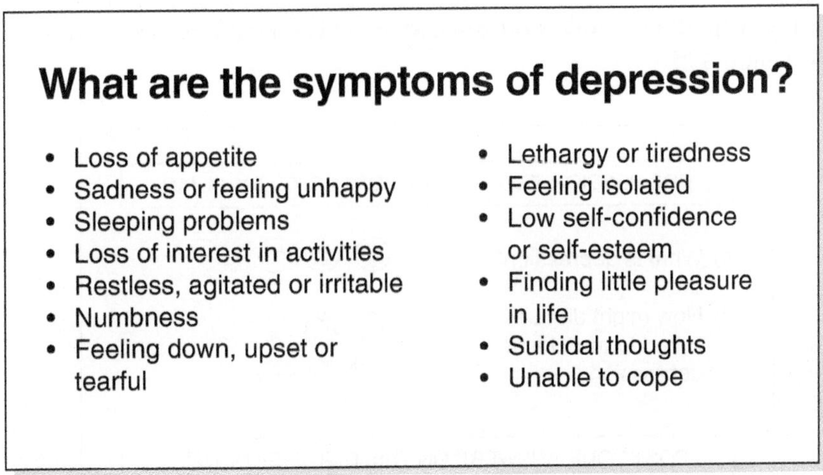

What are the symptoms of depression?

- Loss of appetite
- Sadness or feeling unhappy
- Sleeping problems
- Loss of interest in activities
- Restless, agitated or irritable
- Numbness
- Feeling down, upset or tearful
- Lethargy or tiredness
- Feeling isolated
- Low self-confidence or self-esteem
- Finding little pleasure in life
- Suicidal thoughts
- Unable to cope

Figure 5.1 The first six slides of Simon's original on-campus presentation

From this it can be seen that knowledge can be 'presented' to the student using a wide variety of media. It doesn't all have to be 'told' to them by the teacher – they can be supported to find some of it out for themselves, perhaps as a precursor to a synchronous taught session. In fact, an online environment is ideal for this approach, in part because it allows you to combine some of the approaches described above in order to achieve your learning intentions for your students.

Case study example: *food and mood*

Simon teaches on a third-year undergraduate module called Issues in Food and Nutrition on a Nutrition and Public Health BSc degree course. He has a set of lecture slides on the topic of Diet and Depression which, in the past, he has presented on campus to a group of around 80 students. A decision has been made to 'flip' the face-to-face lecture by changing it into an asynchronous online format. The original lecture lasted two hours and had around 40 slides.

One option is to use a recording of the original lecture in its entirety, but this may not be possible and students may find it hard to follow in this format. Another option is to break the presentation up into sections (what we sometimes refer to as 'chunking') and to consider how to present the information in each section in a way that best enables the student to interact with the content.

Consider the first six slides, as shown in Figure 5.1. We shall call this Section A (note that the slides have been simplified slightly for clarity).

Adapting the slides for an online learning environment

Starting with Slide 2, this short discussion activity could be set in advance (see Figure 5.2).

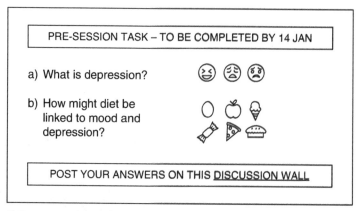

Figure 5.2   Pre-session task

Food and Mood
The impact of diet on mental health

SECTION A – DEPRESSION, CAUSES AND SYMPTOMS

- Please put this presentation into slideshow mode.
- Click to go to the next slide.
- The symbol ◀» means that the slide has an audio commentary.

Food and Mood

SECTION A

Depression, its causes and its symptoms

Learning Outcomes	Define depression Describe the symptoms of depression
Content	What is depression? Symptoms of depression Causes (aetiology) of depression
Self-Completion Tasks (Deadline 25th Jan)	Pre-session Task (5 mins) Video and questions (5 mins) Reading audio-visual slides (5 mins)

Depression

'The common cold of mental illness'

It is estimated that depression will become the second leading cause of disability worldwide by 2020 (WHO, 2012; Lai *et al.*, 2014)

What is depression?

- Click on each of the boxes below to read corresponding definition of depression.
- How does each definition compare to your answers to question (a) on the pre-session task?

MIND (2019)	Thomas (2002)	NICE (2009)

Some symptoms of depression

Compare these with your notes from the video

- Loss of appetite
- Sadness or feeling unhappy
- Sleeping problems
- Loss of interest in activities
- Restless, agitated or irritable
- Numbness
- Feeling down, upset or tearful

- Lethargy or tiredness
- Feeling isolated
- Low self-confidence or self-esteem
- Finding little pleasure in life
- Suicidal thoughts
- Unable to cope

Depression

Talking about Mental Health

- This video from the charity MIND shows a group of people talking about their experiences of depression.

- As you watch the video, note down the symptoms that they describe.

- Remember that you can pause or replay the video if you need to.

Figure 5.3 The same slides but now adapted for asynchronous online use

As an alternative to the two-hour video format, the remaining content in Section A could be presented as a series of 'self-access' slides for the student to work through independently (see Figure 5.3). In this version, the emphasis should shift from the lecturer transmitting the content to the students actively *retrieving* it for themselves.

The following points are of note:

- the slides should be accessible. See Chapter 2 for more on this;
- slide 3 shows the overall purpose and contents as well as the time it should take to work through the activities and the deadline for completion;
- slide 5 has been changed (using the *animation* or *link* functions) so that the student must click on each box to see the definition. This is to increase engagement with the content;
- slide 6 now has a link to a short video, along with a task (slide 7), thus providing an alternative medium and an authentic context for the content. The task is designed to help the viewer interact with the video content.

Other ways to adapt presentation slides for online learning

Here we have 'chunked' the remainder of Simon's original slides as suggested online alternatives as follows:

Table 5.1   Chunked slides

'Chunk' or section of Simon's original slides	Suggested conversion to online learning 'object'	Notes
Diagnosis and risk factors associated with depression	Convert to short video presentation of 5–10 minutes, with slides and audio commentary.	Include questions for the viewer to reflect upon while they pause the recording.
Critical discussion of two research papers	Reading activities related to the two papers.	Students can be asked to read selected extracts and answer key questions, to be discussed in the next synchronous session.
Links between diet and depression (includes complex diagrams)	Animate the slides so that, for example, the different sections in each diagram appear one by one, and add audio commentary.	This provides a multimodal experience which avoids crowding the screen and causing cognitive overload by presenting too much information at once.

(Continued)

Table 5.1   (Continued)

'Chunk' or section of Simon's original slides	Suggested conversion to online learning 'object'	Notes
A set of questions that recap on the content so far	Online quiz with instantaneous feedback as the students submit their answers.	This provides a self-assessment opportunity for the students. The results can also be accessed by the tutor.
Dietary recommendations	These could be converted into handouts in the form of a series of case studies.	Students could be assigned groups and given a case study to prepare notes on and bring to the next synchronous session.

Case study summary

Dividing the content of a two-hour face-to-face lecture into sections – and taking a different approach to the presentation of the content in each section – enables the tutor to create a series of online experiences that support the student to interact with the original lecture content in meaningful, active ways. This then prepares them for a follow-up online synchronous session or a face-to-face taught seminar where they can discuss and apply their newly acquired knowledge.

REFLECTIVE ACTIVITY 5.2

Find a set of slides that you have previously presented as part of an on-campus lecture – say an hour's worth of material – and are likely to be using again but as part of an online asynchronous taught session.

What is the main purpose of the slide content? What do you want the students to take away with them or be able to do by the end of the presentation?

A one-hour video of someone talking about a set of slides can be hard to watch. How can you break up the content of the slides and use different presentation formats and media to make the content more digestible? Divide your slides up into chunks or sections and decide which media will be most appropriate for which section. Use the case study above to generate ideas about your own material, and present your results to colleagues for peer feedback.

Further reading

Ashton, S. and Stone, R. (2018) P is for Presentations. In Ashton, S. and Stone, R., *An A–Z of Creative Teaching in Higher Education*. London: Sage. 113–20.

A short chapter with useful tips for presenting online or face to face.

Mosely, S. (2020) *6 TIPS FOR MASTERING VIDEO PRESENTATIONS*. Blog post. Highfive. Available online at: https://highfive.com/blog/video-presentation-tips (accessed 19 August 2020).

More tips for presenting online.

Reynolds, G. (2011) *Presentation Zen: Simple Ideas on Presentation Design and Delivery* (2nd edn). San Francisco: New Riders.

This includes advice on design as well as performance.

Stone, R. (2020) *I is Also for Informal. How to Ensure that Online Learning isn't Alienating*. Blog post. Available online at: https://anazofcreativeteachinginhe. wordpress.com/2020/05/03/i-is-also-for-informal/ (accessed 29 July 2020).

Lots of ideas for creative ways to enliven your online delivery.

References

Allen, P. and Baughman, F. (2016) Active learning in research methods classes is associated with higher knowledge and confidence, though not evaluations or satisfaction. *Frontiers in Psychology*, 7, 279–86.

Khee, C., Wei, G. and Jamaluddin, S. (2014) Students' perception towards lecture capture based on the technology acceptance model. *Procedia: Social and Behavioral Sciences*, 123, 461–9.

Thomson, A., Bridgstock, R. and Willems, C. (2014) 'Teachers flipping out' beyond the online lecture: maximising the educational potential of video. *Journal of Learning Design*, 7(3), 67–78.

von Glasersfeld, E. (1995) *Radical Constructivism*. London and New York: Routledge Falmer.

6

TEACHING SYNCHRONOUSLY ONLINE

CHAPTER SUMMARY

We begin this chapter with the advantages and disadvantages of teaching synchronously online (that is, live, with the facilitator and participants all present online at the same time), before considering some of the aspects of planning and facilitating online sessions. Two contrasting case studies are included, along with a task to guide the reader through the process of planning their own synchronous online session.

> **REFLECTIVE ACTIVITY 6.1**
>
> Think back to a time when you experienced some synchronous online learning such as a staff training session or a conference webinar. From your perspective as a participant, what were the advantages of it being a synchronous session, as opposed to an asynchronous one (such as a video recording of a lecture, or a reading task)? What were the disadvantages?

Thoughts

Table 6.1 shows some benefits and challenges of synchronous online learning. How do these compare with the ones you came up with?

Table 6.1   The pros and cons of online synchronous teaching

Benefits	Challenges
Participants can interact spontaneously with each other and the facilitator, either by speaking or using a 'chat' function. This social interaction can create a positive learning environment.	If there is a technical problem for a participant – for example, their connection is slow or they can't get their mic or camera to work – they can end up being excluded.
Participants can get immediate feedback or answers to questions.	The more participants you have in one session, the fewer the opportunities for one-to-one tutor interaction with each one. Some may therefore feel ignored.
The facilitator can, to a certain extent, alter the pace or direction of the session according to the feedback from the participants.	Participants may not be able to attend at the time when the session is scheduled, or for the whole session.

In practice, the quality of the teaching and the design of the learning experience can make all the difference. Looking at the challenges in Table 6.1, in a higher education context these could be tackled as follows.

- Teachers can complete an audit of the students' readiness for online learning prior to the first session, including what equipment they have, their internet connection and how confident they are in their use of IT. This includes signposting students to places where they can borrow equipment, apply for an emergency loan, or ask for IT support.
- Students can be supported to feel involved in a synchronous session by using tools such as message boards, breakout rooms and quizzes or

voting software. There are examples of these and other approaches later in this chapter.

- While students should be strongly encouraged to 'attend' synchronous online sessions, they can also be recorded and/or developed into an asynchronous activity for later use.
- For students who miss sessions without informing anyone, follow them up with a phone call. This can be done centrally, but if numbers allow, a personal conversation with the module tutor can go a long way to helping students feel they matter.

What to do when planning synchronous learning

Planning a 'live' (that is, synchronous) session that will be facilitated online is no different from planning any other learning and teaching. Begin with your aims and learning outcomes and select the most effective teaching approaches to support the students to reach those outcomes. This will include any asynchronous tasks that you would like the students to complete prior to or following the synchronous session.

Tools

Chapter 3 has more on this, but video conferencing or webinar tools are the most appropriate for creating a 'live' learning environment, and it's worth talking to the learning technologist team at your institution to find out which ones are supported. You may also wish to draw on supplementary tools such as discussion forums or quizzes. These need to be created in advance and clear links given so that students can access these easily and quickly.

Staffing

Our recommendation is that where possible synchronous online teaching has **two** members of staff present. This is because:

- if one person has technical or other difficulties, the other can take over;
- if there are problems within the group – for example, a student cannot get their microphone to work – one of the teaching team can respond while the other keeps the session going;
- one person can monitor the 'chat' from the students while the other leads the session;
- you can alternate who is the lead facilitator, allowing you both to take breaks;

- you can chip in on each other's presentations; and
- you can peer-review the session with your colleague afterwards.

Of course, there are workload issues here and you may not have been timetabled to teach in pairs. However, if you've turned a two-hour face-to-face lecture into a one-hour synchronous online session along with some related asynchronous tasks then you have saved yourself some direct teaching time before you've even begun.

Timing and breaks

Unlike a face-to-face lecture or seminar, you cannot expect your students to sit still and pay attention for long periods when teaching synchronously online (some would argue that this is the case for face-to-face learning too!). Something that was previously a two-hour lecture or a one-hour seminar will need to be broken down into chunks, with some content turned into asynchronous tasks (such as reading, quizzes, a discussion question) and other parts reserved for the 'live' teaching. Fortunately, as mentioned, splitting the content into synchronous and asynchronous sections will shorten the synchronous part of the session automatically. For example, a long face-to-face lecture could be halved by converting some of the content into self-directed asynchronous activities. But even a 'short' synchronous online session is a big ask. To make this more manageable you will need to build in (a) regular breaks and (b) variety, such as a mix of tutor-led and small-group-led tasks, activities for the students to go off and try themselves before reporting back, and tasks that involve the students communicating with each other, as well as the opportunity to ask questions (Ashton and Stone, 2018).

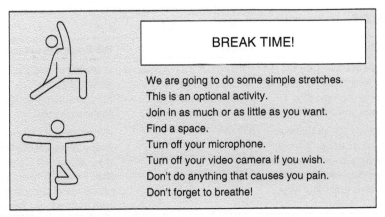

Figure 6.1   Slide about stretching

Breaks really need to occur for at least five minutes every hour, in part because not doing so can lead to neck, shoulder, back, arm and wrist pain or eye strain (HSE, n.d.). During breaks, students should be encouraged to get up, move around, stretch, blink and change eye focus. You can even facilitate some gentle exercises as a group (see Figure 6.1), although it would be wise to consult the wellbeing department at your institution first about which are the most appropriate.

Active learning and feedback

Carrying out a 'traditional' lecture with little or no opportunity for student input is a waste of time in a synchronous learning environment – the students might as well have watched a video of the lecture before arriving. As Lynch (2016, citing Halpern and Hakel, 2003) says:

> The primary take away from research on active learning is that student learning success depends much less on what instructors do than what they ask their students to do.

A session plan for a synchronous teaching event needs therefore to have regular opportunities for students to engage actively with the content and, ideally, with each other. There should also be a clear feedback mechanism for any activities set. Some examples are shown in Table 6.2. Make sure your instructions for such tasks are simple, unambiguous and, ideally, given in spoken and written form. Your activities also need to align with your intended learning outcomes – that is, they should support the students to progress towards achieving these.

Table 6.2 Online active learning ideas

Stimulus	Forum	Feedback mechanism
A simple question such as asking for a definition of a key term or an example of a particular phenomenon. This activity can also be used as an ice-breaker or 'warm-up' task at the start of the session – for example, 'Write down three words to describe your week so far.'	Whole-group synchronous teaching session using a video conferencing tool. Participants answer the question individually and are given sufficient time to reflect upon this and to feed back their answer.	Learners can type their answers into the 'Chat' function within the video conferencing tool. Alternatively, if everyone is happy to use their camera, they can write or sketch their answer in marker pen on a piece of paper and hold this up to the camera!

Stimulus	Forum	Feedback mechanism
A discussion question or practical task to address in small groups, with a time limit and clear instructions about how the results should be reported.	Most video conferencing tools have 'breakout rooms' where you can put people into groups and assign each group a chat room. Here they can talk in private and be visited by the session facilitators.	Feedback could be part of a whole-group plenary, with a representative of each group invited to speak on behalf of the others. You may also wish to make other tools available, such as a message board for the groups to post their responses on.
An example might be: 'List the pros and cons of the research methods used in this report.' Or you could set different tasks for different groups and get them to compare results afterwards.	In our experience, students often find working in a virtual breakout room much less intimidating than speaking out in front of the whole group via the video conferencing tool.	Alternatively, students could use a shared presentation tool (such as Google Slides), each group working on their own slides and then presenting these back to the whole group.
A question asking the student to recall what they know about a particular topic, or to make an argument for a specific viewpoint, or to solve a given problem. This is sometimes known as a three-minute paper (depending on how long you allow for the task).	The question can be posed via the video conferencing tool, but the students can choose their own medium for writing their responses, such as paper and pen. This allows them to take their eyes from the screen and use different muscles, thus providing a short screen break.	Students can be invited to feed back either in the large group, say by inviting people to raise their hands and switch their microphones on, or they could be put in twos or threes in breakout rooms to share their responses to the task, with the teacher(s) dropping in to check progress, followed by a whole-group plenary.

Presenting

In between learning activities and feedback, there may be times where you plan to present some content to the students in a more traditional manner. Video conferencing tools allow you to share presentation slides to the whole group, but it can be tough to present to a laptop screen! Here are some suggestions.

- No student should be forced to turn their camera on if they do not wish to (Bali, 2020), but you can ask them to put a selfie or profile picture on display when their camera is off, so that you at least have an image to present to.

- Pepper your presentation with questions and ask for a show of hands or thumbs up in response (your participants should be able to do this even with cameras off), or single word answers in the chat. Some video conferencing tools also allow students to vote, although you can also use other tools for this such as Kahoot.
- Put the students in pairs in breakout rooms for two minutes and tell them to explain to each other what it is you've just been presenting!
- Keep the presentation elements short and sweet – better to do your presenting in several five- to ten-minute slots, interspersed with questions, quizzes and tasks and even pauses or short breaks, rather than one long 30–40 minute slog where people will tire and lose focus.
- Stop now and again to check what's going on in the chat and respond to it.

What to do when facilitating synchronous learning

The case study below has some tips about managing synchronous teaching and learning events.

CASE STUDY 1: HOW TO RUN AN INTERNATIONAL ONLINE SEMINAR

In 2020, my colleague Judy and I delivered eight webinars via Zoom to groups varying in number between 30 and 300, in 'venues' from Kirklees to Jakarta. This was to support teachers of English for Speakers of Other Languages in facilitating online learning. We shared some slides and we interspersed these with small group discussions in breakout rooms.
  Here are some snapshots of what we learned:

- people need to feel welcome into any space, virtual or otherwise, and to feel 'seen', so we always began in gallery view and greeted as many people as we could as they joined;
- lots of great ideas flooded the chat pane given the right prompts and these were collated and sent out in a PDF after the webinar. Encouraging people to talk to each other via the chat had many benefits, not least that many technical queries were solved by the participants themselves!
- the more 'breakout rooms' we used, the better the feedback. People wanted to be in smaller groups and to talk things over. The only webinar where we couldn't do this was the very large one. Those with 100 or fewer worked fine in small groups and we asked before we set them up that one person type any valuable feedback into the chat pane if there were too many people to do oral feedback;

- technical glitches happen and, after a while, we were more relaxed about a web link not working or being thrown out of a session halfway through. It doesn't happen that often and you just sign back in and try again. Think of it as like those fire alarms which took much longer to recover from!
- we were both working from home and made a feature of this rather than pretending otherwise. For example, we started to ask people to describe the chair they were sitting in as an ice-breaker at the beginning;
- we focused on wellbeing whenever we could and asked people to get up, look out of the window, be kind to themselves. This was hugely popular as many felt pressured by the new normal of working online for hours in a day.

In this way we connected with hundreds of new colleagues across the world, refining our approach with each new session.

Sylvia Ashton

REFLECTIVE ACTIVITY 6.2

Think of a topic that you plan to teach online, and follow these steps.

- Create your intended learning outcomes. What do you want your students to be able to do or to take away from the session?
- What learning activities (including short presentation elements) will best enable your students to achieve your learning outcomes? Which can be designed as asynchronous tasks and which would be more effective if carried out synchronously?
- What tools will you need to run the synchronous part of the teaching?
- How will you staff the session?
- How will you build in breaks and variety?
- Take one of your planned activities. What stimulus will you use to introduce the topic (for example, an image, a question, a problem)? What medium will the students use to carry out the activity? How will they provide feedback?
- How accessible is this activity (See Chapter 2 for more on this)?
- How will you – and the students – assess what learning is taking place?

(Continued)

> Create the necessary resources for your activity, using the appropriate tools, along with an outline plan for the rest of the session, and then try it out on some colleagues. Use their feedback and your reflections to improve your session design.

Thoughts

Planning synchronous online learning is time-consuming. It may be that you keep the design fairly simple at first – for example, by limiting the number of tools used and inviting feedback through basic channels such as the chat function or microphones. Later on, as you become more confident and receive student feedback, you may find that you expand the range of tools used.

Case study 2: a 'jigsaw' discussion

Two lecturers, Ruth and Pranav, taught an online synchronous seminar on a Psychology course. The session was on Equality, Diversity and Mental Health. It was aimed at a group of 30 students. Prior to the session, the

Breakout Room	Discussion Topic / Set Reading	Session Facilitators
Group A	Ethnicity and Mental Health	
Group B	LBTQ+ Young People and Mental Health	
Group C	Poverty and Mental Health	
Group D	Disability and Mental Health	

Figure 6.2   Allocation of groups and reading tasks

students had been split into four groups (A, B, C and D), and each group had been given a different journal article to read. The articles were made available in a format that could be collectively annotated by the group (for example, using Tallis Elevate or similar).

The medium used for the synchronous session was Blackboard Collaborate. While Ruth was introducing the session, Pranav was busy allocating the students to breakout rooms in their groups (A–D), as in Figure 6.2. Each group was asked to briefly discuss the article they'd been assigned, revisiting and reflecting upon their previous shared annotations. While the groups were in their chat rooms, the two lecturers dipped in and out of the discussions, listening and giving feedback.

Following this, the participants were brought back to the main 'room' and given a break, during which Pranav set up new breakout rooms. This time there were six groups, and each group consisted of at least one member from each of groups A, B, C and D, as shown in Figure 6.3.

Breakout Room	Discussion Topics	Session Facilitators
Group 1	Mental Health and • Ethnicity • LBTQ+ Young People • Poverty • Disability	
Group 2	Mental Health and • Ethnicity • LBTQ+ Young People • Poverty • Disability	
Group 3	Mental Health and • Ethnicity • LBTQ+ Young People • Poverty • Disability	
Group 4	Mental Health and • Ethnicity • LBTQ+ Young People • Poverty • Disability	
Group 5	Mental Health and • Ethnicity • LBTQ+ Young People • Poverty • Disability	
Group 6	Mental Health and • Ethnicity • LBTQ+ Young People • Poverty • Disability	

Figure 6.3   Re-allocation of groups and reading tasks

This re-grouping meant that the set reading texts could be compared and contrasted, with the participants reflecting on the implications for the sector as a whole. Pranav and Ruth acted as timekeepers and facilitators, making notes of key points and asking critical questions. In the final part of the session, the students were brought back together for a whole-group plenary to share and reflect on the learning that had taken place.

This approach can be adapted for a number of different subject disciplines – for example, in a science/technology/engineering or mathematics (STEM) session – putting students in breakout rooms and giving each group a different problem to solve, then mixing them up to compare the types of problem and the range of solutions.

Summary

Synchronous online learning provides opportunities for students to interact not just with the teacher but also with each other. A well-designed session will develop not just their collaboration skills but also their communication, and hopefully create a strong learning community in the process.

Further reading

Garnham, W.A. (n.d.) *The Online Active Learning Resource.* Available online at: https://padlet.com/w_a_garnham/7alpdn5vs5yhxhf2 (accessed 2 October 2020).

A Padlet message board, collating ideas for active learning online.

OneHE (n.d.) *Community Building Activities.* Available online at: https://one-heglobal.org/equity-unbound/ (accessed 2 October 2020).

Open educational resources for online community building.

OneHE (n.d.) *Moving HE Teaching Online: Tips, Resources, Support.* Available online at: https://onehe.org/online-teaching/ (accessed 2 October 2020).

Includes a resource bank and an online community with lots of advice about teaching online.

Pearson (2016) *Active Learning. Higher Education Services. White Paper.* Pearson Education. Available online at: https://www.pearsoned.com/wp-content/uploads/INSTR6230_ActiveLearning_WP_f.pdf (accessed 2 October 2020).

A report on active learning in higher education.

Sage (n.d.) *Active Learning in Higher Education*. Journal. Available online at: http:// journals.sagepub.com/home/alh (accessed 2 October 2020, subscription needed).

An international journal for those teaching and supporting learning in higher education. Includes articles on active learning online.

References

Ashton, S. and Stone, R. (2018) *An A–Z of Creative Teaching in Higher Education*. London: Sage.

Bali, M. (2020) *About That Webcam Obsession You're Having* … Blog Post. Available online at: https://blog.mahabali.me/educational-technology-2/about-that-web cam-obsession-youre-having/ (accessed 2 October 2020).

Health and Safety Executive (HSE) (n.d.) *Protect Home Workers*. Available online at: https://www.hse.gov.uk/toolbox/workers/home.htm (accessed 2 October 2020).

Lynch, J. (2016) *What does Research Say about Active Learning?* Pearson Education. Available online at: https://www.pearsoned.com/research-active-learning-students/ (accessed 2 October 2020).

7

TEACHING ASYNCHRONOUSLY ONLINE

CHAPTER SUMMARY

In this chapter we look at some of the factors that need to be considered when designing asynchronous learning. A task on the stages of asynchronous learning design follows, and the chapter concludes with a case study of an asynchronous online collaborative task designed to support students to link theory and practice in their reflective writing.

REFLECTIVE ACTIVITY 7.1

In reading this book, you have effectively been learning asynchronously – that is, in your own time. In relation to this book, then,

1. What have you learned so far?
2. What has helped you to learn?
3. What has hindered your learning?
4. What implications do your answers have for your own students when engaging in asynchronous learning?

Thoughts

Asynchronous learning takes place in your own time. It is an essential component of online learning, given the impracticality of teaching everything synchronously online. Factors that help people to learn asynchronously can be categorised as follows:

- **there may be practical considerations** such as flexible access to the online materials;
- **people's motivations make a difference**, including work-related or personal development goals, or interest in the subject (Guo, 2020; Lind, 2020);
- **accessibility is important** – for example, easy-to-find materials via a well-organised online learning management system (DeNeui and Dodge, 2006). Readability also matters, including the use of multimodal media such as images and text (Ashton and Stone, 2018);
- finally, **the design of the learning matters**, such as pitching the materials at the appropriate level, in a relevant context, with opportunities to practise, consolidate and extend learning.

However, barriers to learning asynchronously can include:

- **lack of time and space**, particularly if working from home;
- **the wrong 'fit'** – for example, the learning is of little relevance or interest;
- **inaccessibility** – for example, the subject is too dry, language is inaccessible, the media used are unimodal (mainly text, for instance), or the content is too theoretical, with few examples from the 'real' world or questions/ tasks to promote reflection;
- **lack of instant feedback or support**, either from the creators of the resource or from peers. This can lead some to feel that asynchronous learning is too 'passive' an experience, which makes it hard to engage with.

These barriers can be addressed in different ways. Below we look at how to consider them as part of the planning of asynchronous online learning.

What to do when planning asynchronous learning

Here are a series of factors to consider when designing asynchronous learning opportunities for an online environment.

Alignment with aims and intended learning outcomes

Having identified a section, 'learning object' or 'chunk' of content for your asynchronous activity, be clear about what you want the students to take from this and how the activity design will support them to make progress in their learning (Biggs and Tang, 2011).

So, for example, if your aim is for the students to apply for ethical approval for a small-scale undergraduate research project, don't send them off reading book chapters and journal articles aimed at postdoctoral researchers. Instead, you could start with abstracts of research studies like those the students are planning, and then get them to identify and share potential ethical issues via a discussion board.

Tools

When planning asynchronous online learning, we have noticed a tendency for academic staff to feel obliged to make a video recording of a lecture (see Chapter 5 for more on this). However, recorded lectures are not the only way to teach asynchronously. One such alternative is a self-access set of slides, where students are asked to open a presentation, put it into slideshow mode and click their way through, slide by slide. At each stage they may be asked to read some content, follow a link to another source, watch a video (embedded in the presentation or signposted) or listen to a sound file/audio commentary. They may also be asked to complete short tasks, such as posting to a discussion forum or solving a problem. Figure 7.1 shows such an example. This format allows you to make content, links and tasks available via one medium. You can make the presentation linear (the student clicks through a slide at a time, completing the tasks as they go) or non-linear (the student chooses from a menu of options and is taken to different parts of the presentation before returning back to the menu again). Creating such a resource can be time-consuming in the first instance, but it can be re-used for subsequent cohorts. It's also easier to update, as you don't need to re-record or re-edit, as you would with a video. The content should be accessible, and all links checked. You can also add accompanying notes (in a format that can be read by screen-reader software).

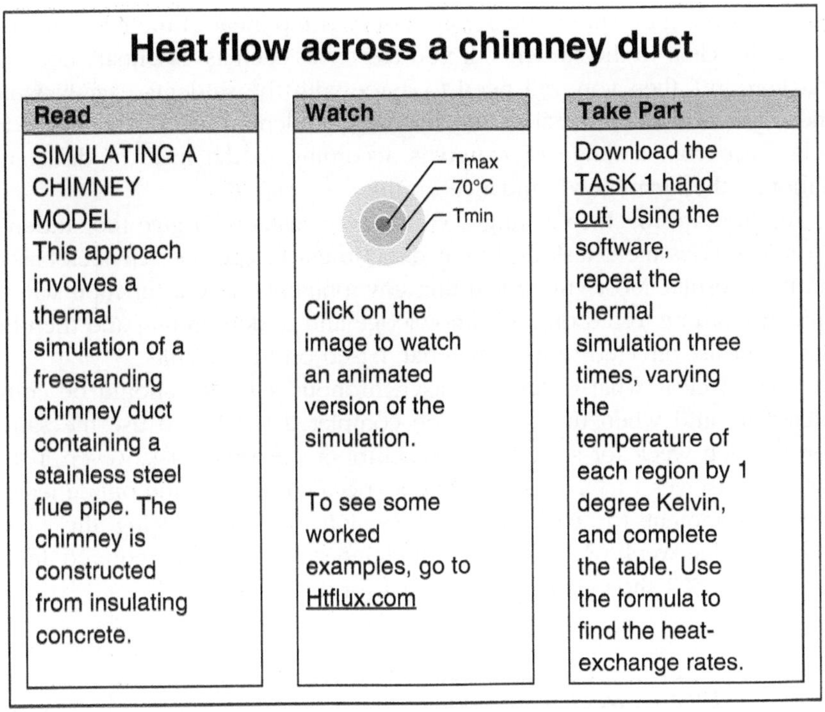

Figure 7.1   Example of self-directed presentation slide. Content adapted from Htflux.com

Other tools for asynchronous online learning include:

- pre-existing videos – why make your own when there may already be one out there that meets your requirements?
- quiz software such as Socrative, Quizlet or Kahoot. Some online learning environments also have their own survey or quiz software built in;
- collaborative documents such as shared slides, word-processing files or spreadsheets;
- set texts – for example, via an online reading list with links to e-versions of literature sources;
- other media such as sound files, images, blogs, vlogs, podcasts and websites, along with questions or tasks designed to support and direct engagement with the content;
- interactive platforms such as social media, discussion forums and message boards.

Essential or optional?

Students can become overwhelmed with too much choice and may feel that they must work through every resource available. Decide whether the task you're working on should be a compulsory component of the learning and make this clear to the students. If you use terms such as 'essential', 'core' or 'background' then you will need to agree with the students exactly what these mean in the context of the learning. Students can also be asked to self-select from a range of materials according to the level of difficulty, although they may need guidance on this.

Another approach to setting asynchronous tasks is to give the students an initial assessment task and then direct them to specific activities based on their results. Most virtual learning environments have a function where students can be tested on their knowledge and understanding and then be automatically directed to new material, based on their results.

Make it clear what order your asynchronous activities should be completed in, and when they should be completed by. Try to use the same format each week for setting the asynchronous learning tasks (even if the tasks themselves vary). This could be a specific folder on the online learning environment for each topic or session, an email listing the tasks expected that week or a document directing students to the required activities. Figure 7.2 shows a possible format for this.

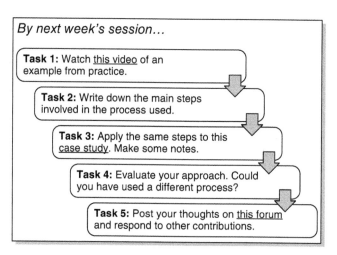

Figure 7.2   Instructions for asynchronous online learning tasks

Finally, explain to the students how they will benefit from engaging with the activity – for example, how the tasks link to the module assessment.

Collaborative or individual?

Many asynchronous learning activities are designed to be accessed individually, at the student's own convenience. However, there may be times when you want the students to work together on a specific task. If this is the case, then it's best to spend some time during a synchronous session doing the following:

- setting up the groups in which you would like the students to work;
- carrying out some 'ice-breaker' activities to build a sense of group cohesion, including negotiating some shared operational guidelines (e.g. 'If you get overloaded with other things and can't meet your personal deadline, let the rest of the group know');
- introducing the task and its purpose, and ensuring that everyone is clear about what they need to do;
- checking that the group understands what the output of the task will be, and how or where they should present it, as well as what their first steps will be;
- directing the groups to the tools that they will need to carry out the task, such as a shared online platform for collaboration, a means of communicating with each other and forms for recording agendas, meeting notes or action points; and
- if needed, assigning specific roles to individuals within each group.

How long you spend on this will depend on the nature and size of the asynchronous task that has been set, whether it will be formatively or summatively assessed and the time period that the students have to complete it. If the task is an ambitious one, you may need to break it down. So, for example, if the students are creating their own online presentations, ask them to outline their aims, objectives and content, and to submit these to you for approval, before they get stuck into design and format decisions.

Assessment

There is more on assessing learning in Chapter 8, but as part of your learning design you will need to consider how you will monitor what learning is taking place asynchronously. This will also include how or when you provide feedback to the students on the results of their assigned tasks, or whether you will create the means for them to self-assess. Some examples are:

- students create a collaborative document which you then comment upon;
- students post to a message board (or via a social media platform) and receive responses from both peers and experts;
- students complete a quiz and get instant, automated feedback on their results;
- students email you with their responses to the activity;

- students vote on the answers to some multiple-choice questions;
- you monitor engagement with the set tasks – for example, via your online learning environment's data analytics, and follow up non-engagers with reminders and encouragement.

Other asynchronous learning design considerations

Whatever medium you are using for your asynchronous learning activities, you will need to consider the following factors.

The **design and accessibility** of the resources, including transcripts or subtitles for videos, alternative text for images, appropriate colour contrasts, use of space and size/type of font, a diversity of contexts and images and so on (see Chapter 2 for more on this). If using slides, contrary to popular opinion, more slides with less use of text on each is better than slides that nearly sink under the weight of the volume of print squeezed onto them.

The use of **different modes of communication** – will you combine images and text, for example? In which case, do the images serve a useful purpose by supporting the text or do they detract (or distract) from it? If you're combining audio and visual input, how will one complement the other (Shams and Seitz, 2008)? Will the use of diagrams clarify or confuse?

Are the **instructions** for any tasks **clear and easy to follow**? Check for ambiguities and, if possible, provide these in more than one format (e.g. audio and visual).

How will you enable the learner to **interact with the content** (for example, by following links, answering questions, being invited to pause and reflect or completing activities)? Are they being asked to read or listen for too long? This can affect concentration and cause participants to tire easily.

Are you building in suggested **breaks** for the learners? Figure 7.3 shows an example from the introduction to a short video, designed to be viewed asynchronously (this was accompanied by an audio commentary).

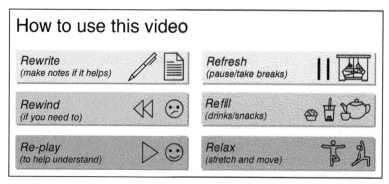

Figure 7.3   Suggestions for students about effective asynchronous learning

Finally, how will you build **additional support** or **extension opportunities** into your asynchronous learning design? Some suggestions are:

- providing the option for students to contact you or another course team member if they have questions about the learning;
- making additional, optional resources available, such as 'hints and tips' hand-outs or links to 'how to' videos (see for example the Khan Academy website (https://www.khanacademy.org/) for how to apply mathematical algorithms);
- enabling peer support by setting up communication channels such as message boards, or by supporting students to set up 'study buddy' groups to learn online together;
- signposting to institutional support such as study skills resources or workshops, or the IT helpdesk (this also applies to pastoral support services);
- setting optional extra reading or tasks for those who wish to study a given topic in more depth;
- directing students to appropriate activities based on initial assessment results.

REFLECTIVE ACTIVITY 7.2

Choose a topic or section of learning that you would like your students to engage with asynchronously and complete the following checklist, following the guidance given above.

1. What will your aims and intended learning outcomes be for the asynchronous activity/activities? How will you enable the students to achieve these?
2. What tools will you use and how will you use them?
3. Will the activities be compulsory or optional? Will there be a deadline?
4. How will you instruct the students on what to do and when to do it by?
5. Will the learning be collaborative or individual? If collaborative, how will you set this up and enable the groups to work in teams?
6. How will students feed back the results of their asynchronous learning? How will you assess their progress and feed back to them?
7. How will you build accessibility into your asynchronous learning design? What about additional support or extension activities?

If possible, get some peer or student feedback on your design plans. You may even wish to develop and pilot some activities and materials.

Case study

This activity was introduced because students on a postgraduate vocational course were struggling with writing a critically reflective essay about their professional practice. Some were focusing on the 'practice' part but not making links to theory, while others were tending to treat the reflective piece more like a literature review, with limited links to practice.

To encourage the students to make more connections between theory and practice in their reflective writing, the activity began with a story, which was first read out by the tutor in a synchronous online session and then made available online in the form of a sound file and accompanying transcript. A shortened version of the story is given below.

'SLIDING FLAWS'

Ali heaved a sigh of relief. The practical observation was over, and it was a 'pass'. Now all that was left was to complete the reflective analysis task. No time like the present, thought Ali, logging onto the laptop. After a slight pause, the tip-tap sound of clicking keys could be heard.

It was around this point, unbeknownst to Ali, that the universe went 'pop' and split into new, multiple versions of itself. This was nothing to worry about, however, as indeed it has been popping and dividing into new universes roughly every millionth of a second from the beginning of time, making every possible outcome a reality, each in its own parallel cosmos.

For example, in universe number 234 291, Ali's cat jumped onto the keyboard and knocked over a cup of coffee in the process. And in universe number 2 000 002, the cat decided to stay under the table, Ali drank the cup of coffee, replied to some emails, played a game of online Scrabble and never actually got around to writing the reflective analysis until the night before submission, culminating in a referral.

But none of these outcomes matter, because it is universes 1 and 2 that we are most interested in. In each of these Ali wrote a reflective analysis essay and submitted it. But they were very different. And each essay was deeply flawed.

Following the story, the students were set a 'quest', which was to read an extract from one of the essays, identify how it could be improved and make two amendments in order to enhance it. The quest was introduced during a synchronous online session using both spoken and written instructions, which were then emailed out to the students following the session. Each student was also assigned a group (A or B) and each group was given a separate link to their assigned essay extract. Table 7.1 shows how the groups were distributed.

Table 7.1   Sliding flaws: how the 'quest' was set up and facilitated

Group	Sample essay	Quest instructions	Tutor's role
A	Sample essay 1 (too much focus on practice and not enough on theory)	Follow the given link to your assigned sample essay extract. Read the extract and rewrite two of the sentences in order to improve the content.	Set up the task (quest), first in the synchronous session and then follow up by email. Monitor the student contributions and chase up those who are not engaging.
B	Sample essay 2 (too much focus on theory and not enough on practice)	Have a look at what your other group members have suggested too and comment on their contributions.	Give feedback in the form of further annotations to the shared essay extracts and invite each group to look at and comment on the work of the other group. Note points to return to in the next synchronous session. Have plenary in the synchronous session to elicit responses to the task and reflect on what learning took place.

What the groups didn't know was that the version 1 of the essay was based entirely on practice, with little or no reference to theory, while version 2 of the essay was largely theoretical in nature, with few links to practice. One group was assigned essay 1 and the other essay 2, depending on what the tutor perceived their learning needs to be. On following the links, students were able to read and annotate their given essay extract. They could do this individually in their own time or arrange with the other group members to work synchronously on the document at a pre-determined time. The groups were given a deadline in terms of when to complete their 'quest'. The tutor visited each group's results and added further comments, as well as emailing those who hadn't yet contributed. The tutor then shared each group's annotated essay extract with the other groups.

In the next synchronous session, the tutor congratulated the students on completing their quests and 'rescuing' the two incomplete essays from universes 1 and 2. The students were given an opportunity to share their thoughts on the exercise and reflect on their own learning in terms of writing their reflective analysis essay.

Summary

The asynchronous task outlined here was a compulsory element of the module. It drew on the principles of storytelling and the idea of a 'quest' as a way of engaging the learners (Ashton and Stone, 2018), and utilised a variety of modes of communication. The adoption of collaborative documents enabled groups to work on the task together (in 'real' time or asynchronously) and the results were then shared and used as a further resource to enable the students to reflect on their own essay writing.

Asynchronous tasks don't necessarily need to be as complex as this. For example, students could complete the activities on their own and then share their results and reflections later. What is important is that any asynchronous learning aligns with the rest of the online course, has a clear purpose and is designed in a way that enables the students not only to reach the intended outcomes but hopefully enjoy themselves in the process.

Further reading

Adams, B. and Wilson, N. (2020) Building community in asynchronous online higher education courses through collaborative annotation. *Journal of Educational Technology Systems*, 49(2), 250–61.

Another case study involving the collaborative annotation of a text, with a focus on how it created a sense of belonging within the group.

Gierach, M., Brechtelsbauer, D., Serfling, J., Bloom, K., Strickland, G. and Heins, J. (2020) Students practicing interprofessional collaboration in the context of hospice and palliative care. *American Journal of Hospice and Palliative Medicine*, 37(12), 1062–7.

This article describes how asynchronous online learning, among other approaches, enabled interdisciplinary collaborative working in a health and wellbeing context.

Stone, R. (2020) *D is for Distance Learning – Part 2*. Available online at: https://anazofcreativeteachinginhe.wordpress.com/2020/04/19/d-is-also-for-distance-learning-part-2/ (accessed 10 October 2020).

This blog post gives some more examples of asynchronous online learning activities, including sorting and matching statements, setting up a virtual 'restaurant' and other creative approaches.

References

Ashton, S. and Stone, R. (2018) *An A–Z of Creative Teaching in Higher Education*. London: Sage. 'V is for Visuals' (159–67) and 'T is for Tales' (144–51).

Biggs, J. and Tang, C. (2011) *Teaching for Quality Learning at University: What the Student Does* (4th edn). Maidenhead: McGraw-Hill/OUP.

DeNeui, D.L. and Dodge, T.L. (2006) Asynchronous learning networks and student outcomes: the utility of online learning components in hybrid courses. *Journal of Instructional Psychology*, 33(4), 256–9.

Guo, S. (2020) Synchronous versus asynchronous online teaching of physics during the COVID-19 pandemic. *Physics Education*, 55(6).

Lind, K. (2020) Mutual aid during a pandemic: a group work class example. *Social Work with Groups (New York. 1978)*, 43(4), 347–50.

Shams, L. and Seitz, A. (2008) Benefits of multisensory learning. *Trends in Cognitive Sciences*, 12(11), 411–17.

8

ASSESSING LEARNING ONLINE

CHAPTER SUMMARY

We begin this chapter with a brief review of formative and summative assessment before looking at some of the types of assessments that work well in online learning, including whether they are suited to formative or summative approaches. We then move on to feedback and some of the ways of providing feedback that align well to online learning. Finally, there is a case study that shows how one teacher changed her practice to make assessment more of a learning experience for her learners, followed by some information about accessible assessment and feedback.

While online learning can allow, or even encourage, us to do things differently, it is often possible to translate practices that work well face to face into online equivalents. Assessment is no different. There are common, established assessment practices (as well as alternatives) that are particularly suited to online ways of working and learning.

Formative and summative assessment

Assessments can generally be categorised as either formative or summative. Formative assessments are those that do not have a bearing on any grade that the learner will receive, rather they are intended as a way for both the learner and teacher to understand the learning that has taken place and identify strengths and further gaps in the learner's knowledge or skills. As they do not have a direct impact on the grade that the learner will receive, formative assessments are often neglected by learners, who prioritise what they see as more important summative assessments (Gardner and Willey, 2012). However, the technologies that support online learning can help make creating, submitting and marking formative assessments much more efficient for both learner and teacher, making them a practical option for gaining an insight into an individual's learning. In addition, through appropriate feedback, summative assessments can also serve a formative purpose.

In addition to more explicit, formal formative assessments there are ways to gain insights into learning that can be used during or between sessions – for example, by questioning learners on their knowledge during a live session. The results of these activities can then be used to adapt the teaching to better suit the collective understanding of the learners – for instance, by moving quickly over material that learners understand well to make more time to cover other material in greater detail. The result of this approach is to provide an experience that is more learner-centric and ultimately learner-directed. An example might be to ask the learners to provide a definition of a key term using the chat function during a synchronous session using a video conferencing tool. The teacher can then build on the learners' responses and address any gaps in understanding.

In contrast, summative assessments are those that directly contribute to the learners' grades and typically serve a more evaluative purpose by 'measuring' learner understanding and performance against set standards. For this reason, they are often larger, more complex pieces of work. Formative assessment tasks can be used to prepare learners for completing their summative assignments. For example, Helen asked her learners to contribute to a discussion forum on 'graduate attributes', reflecting on which qualities they felt confident about and which they needed to develop further. This was in preparation for a module essay in which the learners would be writing about what they had learned on placement. She then gave them feedback on their responses – for instance, asking them to evidence some of their statements using work-based examples. At first, only a handful of learners took up the opportunity to use the discussion forum, but once they realised that they would get detailed responses to their posts and that this would be helpful for their essays, engagement increased.

Summative assessment feedback itself can also bring many of the benefits of formative assessments for assisting learners in both understanding the application of their knowledge and helping direct the learner in further developing that knowledge (Wiliam, 2011). Some courses require learners to keep a portfolio, generally using an online tool, where they record their strengths and areas for improvement from each module assessment feedback report that they receive. They then revisit these at the start of the following module.

Example assessment types

Many types of assessment are suited to online learning, though some adaptation may be required. Some of these are described below and it is also explained whether they are suited to formative or summative assessments, along with whether they can be applied to group work.

Annotated bibliography

An effective way to encourage learners to engage with the academic literature, an annotated bibliography can be an assessment or used as a prelude to a larger piece of work, such as a project or dissertation. The bibliography could be created as an individual task or a group one, potentially even collaboratively between all learners in the cohort. While tools such as Google Docs or Word can be used to produce these bibliographies, more specialised tools such as Diigo or Zotero can make the process more efficient by gathering the required information more easily.

Critique

Often used in the creative industries, the critique offers a way for learners to present their work to teachers and peers and receive feedback and commentary that helps them in further developing their skills and conceptual understanding. Online, this can be conducted as a live activity or over a longer period. Learners can be assessed for the presentation of their own work as well as the quality of the critique that they give to their peers. As a formative exercise, critique can be a very effective method of peer assessment.

Demonstration/walkthrough

Learners demonstrating a technique or showing how an artefact they have created meets a design brief is a common assessment approach and is equally applicable to formative or summative assessment. When working in an online environment, learners may do this by providing a recording for their teacher to watch and later ask questions about, but it could also be done live using an online meeting tool, with the learners either sharing their screen or using the webcam to capture a physical activity, as appropriate. Some meeting tools, such as Zoom, can also allow the teacher to take control of the learner's computer so that they can investigate the on-screen artefact directly.

Discussion

This common learning activity can also be used as an assessment and has the advantage that it can work both synchronously and asynchronously. Synchronous tools, such as Zoom, allow the discussion to be rapid and free-flowing and so allow the teacher to assess how well the learner understands the material being discussed, while asynchronous tools, such as VLE discussion boards, give learners the opportunity to research and craft their contribution over a period of time and so can be used to assess how well the learner can develop and support an argument.

Dissertation/project

Generally, the concluding and most substantial assessment on a course, the project or dissertation allows learners to demonstrate deeper understanding and high levels of skill on a topic of their own choosing. Conducting these as part of online, rather than face-to-face learning may not require many changes, though the learner may wish to use alternative media to present some or all of their work. The regular meetings with a supervisor that typically form a major part of the teacher's input into the learners' activities here can be readily conducted through synchronous meeting tools with learners being able to share their screen to talk through their work.

Essay

A very traditional assessment type, the essay can be used to assess online learning with little change required. However, while standard written essays are the obvious format, online learning lends itself particularly well to alternative, often less text-driven, formats. Ones that work well include blog posts; webpages through tools such as Google Sites or Microsoft Sway; and video/audio recordings. These alternatives can assess the same generic elements, such as development of argument or selection of appropriate references, but give the learners more freedom of expression in their submission and develop their communication skills in a diversity of ways.

In-session quiz

As mentioned in previous chapters, many of the tools used for conducting synchronous sessions have built-in quiz features that can be used to check learners' understanding of material and help inform the direction that the session will take. In addition to these built-in tools, external alternatives with increased functionality, such as Socrative and PollEverywhere, can also be used.

Interview

A learner-initiated and -conducted interview can be an effective assessment type in many disciplines. Through the process of interviewing, the learner can demonstrate their own understanding of their subject while also demonstrating soft skills suitable for the discipline. Interviews could be conducted through online meeting tools or face to face as appropriate, but in either case creating a recording for submission would be straightforward.

Online test

As both a formative and summative assessment approach the online test is highly useful. The ability to offer self-marking tests that learners can take multiple times without needing the teacher to mark and provide feedback means that they are a very valuable formative assessment tool. Additionally, the efficient way that they can be used to mark submissions means they are well suited to summative assessment of large cohorts. They work best for topics where the knowledge is largely uncontested – that is, where the questions have pre-determined, fixed answers – as these can be marked automatically, but more discursive questions can also be used.

Open-book exam

In contrast to face-to-face situations, with online learning it is often difficult, if not impossible, to control the environment in which the learner will sit an exam. While there are technologies that can assist with this, such as by preventing the learners accessing other materials on their computer during the exam or by monitoring them through a webcam, these are not fool-proof and a better approach is to design the exam with the assumption that learners will be able to access additional materials. This is often a better approach anyway because it moves the exam away from testing memory towards testing reasoning and analytical skills.

Portfolio

The portfolio is an excellent way of collating smaller pieces of work into a single package for assessment. Widely used in Arts subjects to showcase a range of different techniques, the same principle can apply in other disciplines, such as collecting and critiquing articles on a range of topics for journalism or presenting several smaller programs as a package in software engineering. The items within the portfolio could also be different formats, such as text, video, audio, or images, as required. A commentary drawing the collection into a coherent whole is a common element of a portfolio. While there are dedicated portfolio tools, such as PebblePad and Mahara, and many virtual learning environments have a relevant feature, portfolios can also be created and shared as blogs or webpages.

Poster

Producing a poster is an effective and creative way for learners to give a summary of a topic or piece of research. The need to effectively communicate within a constrained space or format encourages learners to consider the most salient points of their work and how best to articulate them. While traditional desktop publishing or design software can be used to produce the poster, online infographic tools such as Canva and Piktochart offer more visual and engaging ways to present data.

Presentation

Another common form of assessment, presentations work very well as online assessments because they can use the same tools that are used for teaching. The presentations could be delivered live or as pre-recorded videos, and groups of learners can use editing tools such as Google Slides or Microsoft Office365 to create slides collaboratively.

Research/project proposal

Setting a research or project proposal as an assessment provides a way to encourage learners to prepare for a larger piece of work while also receiving feedback that will help direct their efforts on that piece of work. Depending on the requirements of the subsequent work, the proposal could take the form of a written proposal, but alternative formats such as a 'talking head' video can be very effective.

Viva/oral exam

The viva voce, or oral exam, is the predominant method used in the defence of doctoral theses, but also has wide application in other assessment, from assessing spoken language abilities through to verifying that the learner is the author of their other submitted work. This approach works well online as online synchronous meeting tools, such as Zoom or Skype, can be used to facilitate the same questioning and probing of the learner's knowledge almost as effectively as the face-to-face equivalent. These same tools would also enable the learner to deliver a live presentation should that be part of the assessment.

ACTIVITIES

1. Select an online learning activity that you have created. This can be asynchronous or synchronous. How might you incorporate formative assessment and feedback into the design, so that you and your learners gain a better understanding of their learning?
2. Consider the summative assessment task for a module that has previously been taught face to face. How might you redesign it for an online environment?

EXAMPLES

The following examples each show one way that the above questions can be addressed.

ACTIVITY 1

A simple example is, during a synchronous presentation, for the teacher to put everyone in breakout rooms in pairs for a minute (with warning!) and say, 'Now explain to each other what I just said.' When the learners return to the main presentation, they can share how effectively they were able to do this and report any gaps in their understanding. This approach combines self-, peer and teacher assessment.

ACTIVITY 2

Imtiaz needed to adapt a face-to-face peer-assessed presentation-based assignment into an online alternative. He got each group to create a short video presentation instead and then sent the learners formal invitations to the premiere showings (Figure 8.1). After each viewing, the learners were asked to post their feedback on a shared discussion forum.

Figure 8.1   Formal assessment invitation to learners

The role of feedback

Assessment, whether formative or summative, is an important part of the learning process, but without feedback to guide learners on what they did and did not do well it can only have a limited effect on learning. There is often disagreement between what a teacher considers to be good feedback and what a learner considers it to be. Teachers often view feedback as something that can help the learner in regards to the exact piece of work on which the feedback has been given as well as providing guidance on how to improve future work more generally, known as 'feedforward' (Baker and Zuvela, 2013). However, learners often seem to focus on the former at the expense of the latter. This can lead to learners making little use of feedback when they feel that the sole purpose for which it would have been useful, the original assessment, has already been completed (Hepplestone et al., 2016).

Feedback can be provided to learners at different levels, or a combination of them, as appropriate.

- **Individual** – this is the typical level of feedback where learners will each receive personalised commentary on their own work. It offers the greatest ability to direct learners' understanding of their own work but is also the most time-consuming approach as each learner needs their own personalised feedback. Most traditional techniques for giving individual feedback translate well to online learning yet can be supplemented or replaced with alternatives only practical through electronic means.
- **Collective** – providing feedback to all learners on common aspects or errors seen across multiple learners' submissions can be more efficient than repeating the same feedback to many individuals. This could be as general commentary, but could also take the form of worked examples, where appropriate. While this approach can be effective, it is best suited as a supplement to personal feedback rather than a replacement. Figure 8.2 shows such an example in a 'newspaper' format, but other formats can be used, including podcasts or slides.
- **Peer** – a common approach to feedback in massive open online courses where the number of learners would make individual feedback from teachers impossible, this can also be used in situations with more manageable numbers of learners. When used on an appropriate assessment it offers a way for learners to reflect on their own work by analysing how other learners approached the same brief.

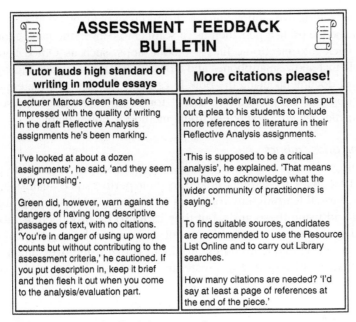

Figure 8.2   Assessment feedback 'newspaper'

Types of electronic feedback

Written comments and annotations

Written feedback can usually be made against an entire submission through the virtual learning environment, but it is often possible to also add comments and annotations into individual files too. Features such as Comments and Track Changes in Microsoft Word or the Sticky Notes and Highlighter in PDF software can enable this type of feedback even when a virtual learning environment is not being used. Although these will appear as written text, the dictation tools mentioned in Chapter 2 can allow these to be made by speaking rather than typing.

Handwritten annotations

If you have access to a tablet, such as an iPad, or a graphics tablet like those used by illustrators, then you may also be able to provide handwritten feedback on files submitted electronically. Whether this approach is possible will depend on the type of file that has been submitted, but the ability to hand annotate documents is built into Word and PDF documents, and image files naturally lend themselves to being annotated in this way. As with any situation where handwriting is being used, it is important to be careful to ensure that the results are clearly legible. A possible, though less practical, alternative annotating electronically would be to print out the work, annotate using a pen, then use a scanner to convert the hand-annotated pages back into electronic files – mobile apps, such as Office Lens, are available that allow smartphones and tablets to be used to create high-quality 'scans' of documents using the built-in camera. This use of an intermediary hard copy can be particularly useful for complex annotations, such as mathematics, when a solely electronic method is not available.

Marking grids/rubrics

Marking grids, also known as rubrics, offer a fast way to provide standardised feedback to learners linked to their performance against defined criteria. Virtual learning environments often provide functionality for producing and using these grids, but they can also be produced as tables in a word processor or a spreadsheet tool. The main advantage to using the tool from the virtual learning environment is that it removes much of the file management required to create and distribute rubrics to the correct learner.

Audio feedback

As an alternative to written feedback, an audio recording can be given to learners instead. This can be quicker to produce and more detailed as most people speak faster than they type and – because it has clearly been made specifically for them, rather than put together from standard written phrases – learners generally find it more personal and informative. A major contributor to this more personal feel is that tone of voice can be used to add an additional layer of meaning to what is being said. However, it is important to remember that, unlike annotations, the audio will not be linked directly to parts of the submission and this loss of context may make the feedback less useful to learners. Audio can be recorded with software on a computer, such as the free Audacity tool, as well as with a mobile device.

Screencast feedback

Using a screencasting tool, the learner's electronically submitted work can be shown while providing commentary. This gives the benefits of audio feedback, in that it is more personal and often quicker to produce than written feedback, while also making clear the link between specific comments and the part of the submission to which they relate. Both screencast and audio feedback can be produced while looking at the submission for the first time, but better results are usually obtained by making the recording after having looked at the entire submission first. Screencasts and audio feedback can both be used to supplement written feedback or annotations, as well as replacing them. This approach is popular with some learners, as it feels like a personal tutorial.

Video feedback

Like audio and screencast feedback, video feedback can be more engaging and feel more personal. This approach is particularly suited to assessments that involve a physical dimension, such as the demonstration of a technique or a physical or printed artefact, rather than an electronic file or document. A video camera, smartphone or webcam can be set up to record the teacher demonstrating the correct technique or exploring the physical submission while providing commentary.

Automated feedback

As described earlier, depending on the question types used, online quizzes and tests can be efficient ways of providing feedback because feedback can be created in advance for different answers and for the overall result. The tool will then take care of providing the feedback to learners based on their responses. This approach is particularly well suited to formative assessments that enable the learners to test their own understanding because, once set up, the learners can take the test multiple times and so check their understanding whenever they wish with no further impact on the teacher's time. With some quiz software you can also add explanations into the feedback, which can help learners to address any gaps in understanding or knowledge (see Figure 8.3 for an example).

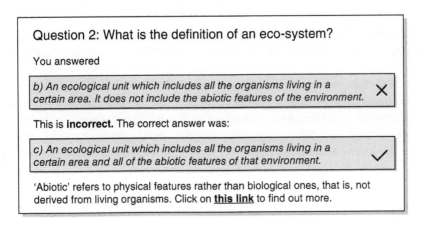

Figure 8.3 Automated quiz feedback example

Live feedback

The above methods of providing feedback involve pre-preparing feedback for the learner to access later; however, synchronous methods of providing feedback are also possible online. These would use the same tools that are used for synchronous teaching and could be delivered to learners collectively or individually just as they would be with face-to-face teaching.

This approach has the advantage that the feedback and any related discussion can easily be recorded, meaning that the learners can later review exactly what was said.

Case study

Pek Yin teaches Fine Art and had assessed learners' artwork using a critique-based approach for several years. However, while other learners have always been invited to observe these sessions, the actual marking and feedback has always been conducted by Pek Yin and attendance has often been low at these sessions. Seeing that learners can gain a lot of insight into their own artwork by attending the critique of their peers, Pek Yin decided to incorporate peer participation in the assessment critiques by allocating 10 per cent of the final marks to the learners' personal reflection on the peer feedback they received. To help direct the learners' contributions towards the relevant aspects of the assessment, Pek Yin created an online feedback and marking grid for the learners to complete when assessing their peers as well as a template to guide the reflection. As the feedback template was already online, to support her learners with anxiety about presenting their artwork Pek Yin gave the learners the option to present their work and receive their peer feedback either synchronously in a face-to-face session, or asynchronously by recording their presentation instead.

Initially, Pek Yin found that the learners struggled with both tasks, particularly giving constructive feedback to their peers. However, following refinement of the way that she introduced the tasks, the quality of critique and reflection improved and it became clear that learners were learning about their own work and the entire assessment process through the activity. Although it is difficult to quantify, Pek Yin felt that the overall quality of work is improved after going through this peer critique process, partly because learners have a better understanding of how their work is assessed and a mark obtained.

REFLECTIVE ACTIVITY

Think about feedback that you have given in the past, either formal or informal, as part of a face-to-face learning environment. To what extent might your approach to feedback need revising in the context of an online environment? How might you use some of the approaches in this chapter to enhance the feedback experience for the learner?

Inclusive assessment and feedback

Having looked at some of the different assessment types and feedback formats, it should be clear that online learning offers significant flexibility for both teacher and learner. It is this aspect that forms one of the foundations of inclusive assessment and feedback practice – the opportunity to use alternative methods based on preference and need. For example, a learner who feels severe anxiety about presenting in front of people may be able to pre-record their presentation for later playback, which could help them perform better than would be the case in live delivery. The online environment can also make accommodating the particular requirements of learners easier, such as simplifying arranging a sign language interpreter during a live, assessed presentation when the signer only needs to access the online tool rather than attend a physical space. The wide variety of tools and formats that are available online makes it possible to give learners additional freedom in how they create their submissions, so some may choose to populate their reflective portfolio with written pieces, while others might present their work visually or as video diaries.

With feedback, the choice of format can be used to aid the learner in interpreting the information. So, for the same assessment a dyslexic learner might get their feedback as an audio file while a deaf learner would receive written feedback. In this way, the feedback is adapted to the learner's needs yet would still be able to convey the same richness of information.

Further reading

https://academic.shu.ac.uk/assessmentessentials (accessed 17 October 2020).

Sheffield Hallam University's Assessment Essentials *provides information on the full assessment cycle, including specific information for online assessments.*

https://www.ucl.ac.uk/teaching-learning/sites/teaching-learning/files/self_and_peer_assessment.pdf (accessed 17 October 2020).

Higher Education Academy's Self- and Peer-Assessment Guide for Biosciences *has advice on a range of assessment types and is applicable beyond the stated discipline.*

https://anazofcreativeteachinginhe.wordpress.com/2018/11/12/f-is-also-for-feedback-and-feelings/ (accessed 21 October 2020).

A brief look at how feedback can positively and negatively affect learners, their motivation and emotions.

References

Baker, D.J. and Zuvela, D. (2013) Feedforward strategies in the first-year experience of online and distributed learning environments. *Assessment and Evaluation in Higher Education*, 38(6), 687–97.

Gardner, A. and Willey, K. (2012) Student participation in and perceptions of regular formative assessment activities. In Mann, L. and Daniel, S. (eds), *23rd Annual Conference of the Australasian Association for Engineering Education 2012: Profession of Engineering Education: Advancing Teaching, Research and Careers*. Melbourne: Engineers Australia. 58–67.

Hepplestone, S., Glover, I., Irwin, B. and Parkin, H. (2016) Setting out the role of feedback in the assessment process through both the student and tutor perspective. *Practitioner Research in Higher Education*, 10 (1), 81–90.

Wiliam, D. (2011) What is assessment for learning?. *Studies in Educational Evaluation*, 37(1), 3–14.

9

FURTHER IDEAS AND EXAMPLES

CHAPTER SUMMARY

In this chapter, we begin with some ideas for warm-up games, after which we consider other creative teaching approaches such as avatars, comics and gamification. We also look at ways in which to disrupt more traditional methods. Some of the examples are taken from outside the university context. We hope that you can find ways to adapt them for your own teaching. Remember also that you can create opportunities for your students to design and employ their own resources and activities.

Warm-ups

Warm-ups or 'ice-breaker' activities can help students to engage not only mentally but emotionally. They can reduce anxiety; establish teacher–student and student–student rapport; build a learning community; encourage cooperation and generate feelings of belonging (Johnson, 2012). This is even more important in an online learning environment, where there is more potential for students to feel invisible and inaudible. Thanks to friends, students and colleagues for the three examples below.

Instant poetry

Each person is asked to write down a word or short phrase to describe a positive moment that they have experienced in the last week, and then hold their results up to their camera. Using the 'gallery' view, someone reads out the words and phrases in the order in which they see them, thus creating an instant, co-created poem (see Figure 9.1 for an example).

Figure 9.1   Instant online poetry

Wiki-race

Someone chooses two completely unrelated items at random, say *potatoes* and *ice-skating*, and then shouts 'Go!' Each participant opens Wikipedia and types in one of the words (e.g. *potato*). They must then arrive at the Wikipedia page for the other word in as few steps as possible, by clicking on intermediate linking words. In the above example, the Wikipedia entry for *potato* lists the *United States of America*. Clicking on this and scrolling down the Wikipedia entry for the USA, we find *Sports* and then *Winter Olympics*, and the entry for this, of course, has a link for *ice-skating*. The first person to find a path from one of the two chosen words to the other shouts 'Bingo!' They must then explain the 'route' they took through the Wikipedia pages. Conducting what is essentially a race in real time can have the effect of energising the group and creating a sense of competition.

Scavenger hunt

Check that the students are all in their own homes, then give them a short list of items to find (see Figure 9.2 for some examples) and set a time limit, say, three minutes. When the students return, put them into breakout rooms and get them to share their treasures with each other on camera. This game can help to build trust and communication, and it has the added bonus of getting the students up and moving. Be careful about students who may be anxious about putting their cameras on or have mobility issues, and provide an optional alternative task.

SCAVENGER HUNT

Find

1. a favourite mug,

2. something blue,

3. something soft,

4. a photo and

5. an ornament

YOU HAVE THREE MINUTES!

Figure 9.2   Scavenger hunt instructions

An internet search will bring up multiple suggestions for other online warm-ups.

Avatars, comics and gamification

In this section we look at how to adopt different elements of computer games to enhance student engagement when learning online.

Avatars

Populating slides or webpages purely with content can lead to a soulless learning experience. Creating an avatar to take on the role of a coach can make the virtual environment a friendlier, more informal space. Such a character can act as presenter, guide, questioner, or adviser. They can also be used to model or demonstrate techniques or problem-solving approaches (Clark and Mayer, 2017). Employing more than one avatar means that different characters can serve different purposes. Figure 9.3 provides an example of the use of an avatar.

Figure 9.3   Using an avatar

There are many websites and apps that can help you to create avatars, but before designing your list of characters, there are some decisions to make. Table 9.1 lists some of the possibilities.

Table 9.1   Decisions to make about your avatar

Medium	Appearance	Speech	Role
• Series of drawings • Animated/still • Photographs of a real person • Videos of a real person • Puppet	• Comical or caricatured • Human or other • Smart or casual • Other factors such as age, ethnicity, gender, disability, size, etc.	• Printed text • Voice recordings (audio narration) • Computer-simulated voice • Speech bubbles	• Virtual instructor • Guide to the content • Question-poser • Feedback-giver • Top tips presenter • Case study • Character in a story • Fellow student

The most important aspect of creating avatars to support online learning is keep your overall design simple; avoid gimmicks such as gifs, sound effects, music and so on. The avatar should exist to enable the learners to achieve the intended outcomes, not simply to entertain or, worse, to distract them. As such, they should therefore be relatable to the target audience and avoid stereotypes or clichés. The second most important aspect is to pilot the use of your avatars before designing them into a whole course; listen to your students' feedback. Research findings on the use of avatar-instructors in online learning are mixed, with some studies reporting no difference in student performance and others indicating improved performance and higher levels of enjoyment when on-screen agents are used (Dey *et al.*, 2009).

Choose your own comic book ending

Presenting knowledge in comic strip form is a novel way of engaging students' attention. Designing an online comic book where the viewer gets to

Figure 9.4 Comic about choosing a research topic *These images were created at MakeBeliefsComix.com; go there to make your own comic strips.*

choose how the story ends is even more appealing. There are a number of websites that can support you to create your own comics, including backgrounds, characters, expressions and speech bubbles. To enable the viewer to choose their own ending, you can cut and paste the comic into a series of presentation slides, sections of which can then be hyperlinked to other slides, depending on which choices the viewer selects. This is time-consuming to create, but the resulting resource can be used again and again.

Here's an example of a story about a character called Zara, a student on placement in a school who is choosing a research topic for her module assignment (see Figure 9.4). The comic was introduced in a synchronous online session, with the students debating the pros and cons of each of Zara's choices. Having heard all the arguments, each student then decided which topic Zara should go for and clicked on their choice to find out what happened next. This led them along one of four different storylines, where Zara discovered the advantages and disadvantages of trying to research the topic in question. Finally, at the end, the students reviewed the choices they'd made and voted on the topic they believed to be the most researchable.

The activity was successful, with the students enjoying the novelty value of the comic book format and having the ability to change the ending. The combination of images and words aided their understanding and held their attention (Mayer, 2001). They applied their knowledge of what makes a topic 'researchable' and used this to predict the best outcome for Zara. And they were able to test their hypotheses by selecting the appropriate ending and finding out how Zara got on.

It is worth noting that Zara is an example of how an avatar can be used as part of a longer story or scenario in order to support learning. Also, in this story, the protagonist was simply another student. The 'real' students, however, by engaging with Zara's journey, effectively became teachers or guides themselves.

Gamification

Gamification refers to the use of game mechanics, such as leaderboards, rewards and clearly defined goals, to motivate learners while helping them in directing their effort and time. Gamification works by tapping into people's competitive and/or cooperative instincts to encourage participation and scaffold learning and is particularly suited to formative and 'optional' activities (Glover, 2013). Gamification can be used at a range of different levels, from individual activities through to module or even course level. However, while gamification can be beneficial for many learners, it is not without its potential problems. In particular, the addition of a layer of extrinsic motivation – that is, making achievement and learning more publicly visible – can dissuade already well-engaged learners with high intrinsic motivation from participating. A further issue is that, without careful planning, a larger scheme of gamification can encourage some learners to spend too much time on less important activities because they are an easy way to boost their standing on a leaderboard rather than moving onto more important and challenging activities. Yet, despite these potential limitations of gamification it can offer real benefits for learners, and for teachers it provides an opportunity to think about how to scaffold learning on both a small scale and a larger one.

For an example of how gamification might be applied, an area that is often challenging is groupwork. This is a good area for applying gamification because learners are often reluctant to work together when they feel they put in more effort for reduced benefit, seeing other learners perhaps as 'freeloaders'. By gamifying the groupwork activity, students can obtain recognition and reward for the effort they put into collaborating with peers and, with careful consideration, specific types of collaboration can be encouraged. A suitable mechanism for this is digital badges, where members of each group could nominate their peers for particular badges based on their contribution to the work. For example, there could be a badge available for the greatest contribution to researching the topic, another for developing the presentation, one for developing the report and one for overall contribution. The learners could then nominate other group members for each badge and the one with the most votes from their groupmates would receive that badge. The learners would be able to add the digital badges to online portfolios and use them as evidence of group working skills for prospective employers, making obtaining a badge a desirable objective.

Other creative (and disruptive) approaches

Defamiliarising the familiar is a phrase used in relation to qualitative research (Mannay, 2010). It's about the phenomenon of taking our environment for granted and, as a result, inadvertently closing our minds to new ways of seeing things. Thus, students who are fed a diet of the traditional 'lecture/demonstration-followed-by-application' routine can become numbed to deeper insights and fresh perspectives, and subsequently adopt a 'surface' approach to their learning (Entwistle and Ramsden, 2015). Online learning can offer an opportunity to embrace innovative and unexpected ways of introducing new knowledge.

Pets, places, children and washing machines

One way of breaking the monotony of a filmed presentation is to allow yourself to be human – for example, introducing your cat or your family to your students, apologising for the noise of the washing machine or going for a walk and filming yourself talking in different locations. Students tend to respond positively to these departures from the formality of a traditional lecture, as they are a reminder that their teacher is also an ordinary person with conflicting demands on their time.

Stories, role-play and enactments

Documentary maker Saskia Wilson has this to say about using narrative structures to engage students in learning:

> *In terms of documentaries, the biggest way of holding attention is through compelling storytelling. So, often you have a tease of the subject at the start of a documentary, e.g., on tv it's some highlights of what's to come, but it could be a question or a powerful scene that hooks you into the subject or setting out with an engaging character. Then it's about structuring the information so you're always finding out a little bit more and piecing things together.*

(Wilson, 2020)

On an 'Empowering Parents Empowering Communities' online parenting course (Penney *et al.*, 2010; Day *et al.*, 2012), the trainer set up some cuddly toys, a jug of water and some glasses. She explained that each toy was a child and that the jug held the parent's resources. The participants were invited to give examples of the children's everyday needs (*I feel sick! Where's my PE kit?* And so on). For each example, the trainer poured some water from the jug into one or other of the glasses. Pretty soon the jug was empty; the trainer explained that the resources of the parent were now depleted. She asked the participants what the parent could do to 'top up' their resources (such as making time for oneself or talking to friends). Each time a suggestion was made, the trainer refilled the jug a little, this time using fruit cordial as a contrast. The exercise provided a powerful reminder of the importance of self-care.

Human brains are hardwired not only to look for novelty but also to *seek connections to previously stored information and constantly search for personal meaning* (Johnson, 2012: xviii). Using everyday props, analogies and stories can support learners to make these connections. Examples might include a balloon to illustrate the nature of capitalism or a box of buttons to demonstrate ratios or groupings in a particular scenario or context. Having a camera close means that you can exploit the fine detail of the props you're using, such as necklaces or chains that can be manipulated to represent levels of protein structure (Tamari *et al.*, 2015). And, of course, you can encourage your students to explain concepts and processes using their own props and scenarios.

Windows, walls and tablecloths

In the film *A Beautiful Mind*, the mathematician John Nash, played by Russell Crowe, is seen writing mathematical equations on glass window-panes, presumably because the filmmakers felt that pen and paper was too dull a medium. The same technique was employed by Rowena, an online learning designer, when tasked to show different methods of calculating a weekly wage from an hourly one, as part of an 'Everyday Maths' MOOC. She made a film where people were stopped in the street and asked how they would work out someone's weekly income from a set of given figures. They then showed their 'working out' using a grease pen on a shop window. Some of the participation was staged, but some were genuine passers-by (including some local builders who commented that the given rate of pay was too low!). We're not suggesting you film on location and hire a cast of actors to make videos, but you can disrupt familiar routines by using different media to present examples or explanations, including writing on paper tablecloths or on flipchart paper stuck to the wall. Doing so can provide a sense of spontaneity, it allows you to present in real time rather than via a somewhat flat and lifeless 'here's one I did earlier' example on a PowerPoint slide, and it enables you to use diagrams, symbols and word clouds as well as text. Care must be taken that the content is fully accessible, however – for example, making sure the lighting is adequate and providing an audio commentary alongside the visual element. Similar media can also be used by the students themselves – for example, allocating breakout rooms and assigning each group a drawing task using pen, paper and shared cameras. The key is in varying the approaches used in order to prevent the numbness that comes with repetition and routine.

REFLECTIVE ACTIVITY

Choose an example that you like from this chapter (or indeed, elsewhere in the book) and adapt it for your own subject discipline and context. If possible, trial the learning activity on a colleague or on some friendly students. Use their feedback to improve on the design and accessibility of the resource.

Conclusion

Making space for spontaneity and creativity as well as mixing low-tech and high-tech approaches can provide variety and entertainment for your students, as can drawing on metaphors, multimodal media and humour to enhance learning (Ashton and Stone, 2018). A balance needs to be sought, however, between being too 'gimmicky' and thus detracting from the intended learning outcomes, on the one hand, and becoming too 'dry' and losing students' attention, on the other. Eliciting feedback from students means that you can evaluate and revise your approaches as you go along, while staying true to your intended outcomes will keep the learning focused and clear.

Further reading

Warm-ups and ice-breakers

Korsunskiy, E. (2020) *Zoom-Friendly Warmups and Icebreakers*. Future of Design in HE. Available online at: https://medium.com/future-of-design-in-higher-educa tion/zoom-friendly-warmups-and-icebreakers-3400c8b7263 (accessed 13 November 2020).

Smart, J. (2020) *20 Online Energisers for Virtual Teams and Remote Meetings*. SessionLab. Available online at: https://www.sessionlab.com/blog/online-energizers/ (accessed 13 November 2020).

Comics and avatars

Kessler, S. (2018) *4 Free Sites for Creating Your Own Comics*. Mashable UK. Available online at: https://mashable.com/article/create-your-own-comics/?europe=true (accessed 13 November 2020).

Pappas, C. (2014) *Top 10 Tips on How to use Avatars in eLearning*. eLearning Industry. Available online at: https://elearningindustry.com/top-10-tips-use-avatars-in-elearning (accessed 13 November 2020).

Gamification

Owen, J. (2018) *Gamification: Still a Hot Trend in Education?* Education Technology. Available online at: https://edtechnology.co.uk/comments/gamification-still-a-hot-trend-in-education/ (accessed 13 November 2020).

Creative and disruptive ideas

Stone, R. (2020) *D is also for Distance-Learning Part 2. How to Help Your Students to Engage with Each Other*. Available online at: https://anazofcreativeteaching-inhe.wordpress.com/2020/04/19/d-is-also-for-distance-learning-part-2/ (accessed 13 November 2020).

References

Ashton, S. and Stone, R. (2018) *An A–Z of Creative Teaching in Higher Education*. London: Sage. Chapters E and V.

Clark, R. and Mayer, R. (2017) *E-learning and the Science of Instruction: Proven Guidelines for Consumers and Designers of Multimedia Learning* (4th edn). Hoboken, NJ: Wiley.

Day, C., Michelson, M., Thomson, S., Penney, C. and Draper, L. (2012) Evaluation of a peer-led parenting intervention for child behaviour problems: a community-based randomised controlled trial. *British Medical Journal*, 344(13 March).

Dey, E., Burn, H. and Gerdes, D. (2009) Bringing the classroom to the web: effects of using new technologies to capture and deliver lectures. *Research in Higher Education*, 50, 377–93.

Entwistle, N. and Ramsden, P. (2015) *Understanding Student Learning (Routledge Revivals)*. Abingdon: Routledge. (First published in 1983 by Croon Helm.)

Glover, I. (2013) Play as you learn: gamification as a technique for motivating learners. In Herrington, J., Couros, A. and Irvine, V. (eds), *Proceedings of World Conference on Educational Multimedia, Hypermedia and Telecommunications 2013*. Chesapeake, VA: AACE. 1999–2008.

Johnson, L. (2012) *Kick-Start Your Class: Academic Icebreakers to Engage Students*. San Francisco: Jossey-Bass.

Mannay, D. (2010) Making the familiar strange: can visual research methods render the familiar setting more perceptible? *Qualitative Research*, 10(1), 91–111.

Mayer, R. (2001) *Multimedia Learning*. New York: Cambridge University Press.

Penney, C., Draper, L., Kearney, C., Adewole, C. and Day, C. (2010) *Being a Parent. Empowering Parents, Empowering Communities: Parenting Group Manual*. South London and Maudsley NHS Foundation Trust/King's College, London/ Parenting Centre, Surrey.

Tamari, F., Bonney, K. and Polizzotto, K. (2015) Prop demonstrations in biology lectures facilitate student learning and performance. *Journal of Microbiology and Biology Education*, 16(1), 6–12.

Wilson, S. (2020) Private email correspondence.

10

TROUBLESHOOTING

CHAPTER SUMMARY

In a perfect world our internet connections would never fail, there would be no power cuts, learners would always be happy to undertake activities and everyone would have comprehensive digital skills. Unfortunately, the real world is quite different from this. In this chapter we look at some issues that might arise and how they might be addressed, both technical problems and those that relate more to people. Unlike the other chapters in this book, we have not included a reference section in this chapter, since most of the content is based on our combined professional experience. There are, however, some further reading suggestions at the end.

Introduction

'Fall down seven times, get up eight,' says the Japanese proverb. The first thing to say about teaching online is that things will not always go to plan, but that this should not put you off trying new approaches and tools. When things do go wrong it is important to stay calm and address the issue without panicking. In this chapter we will cover some ways to help ensure that you can adapt to unplanned changes and continue to provide a positive experience for your learners.

At the risk of oversimplifying, there are two broad categories of issues that you might encounter: those that relate to technology and those that relate to people. It is likely that over time you will encounter both types, but despite the technical issues often seeming the most daunting they can generally be addressed relatively easily, whereas issues related to people can be significantly harder to resolve because there is seldom a single common cause for such issues. However, in both cases, anticipating some of the issues that you might face and working out what you can do to limit the impact, either in advance or when the problem occurs, will help to keep your teaching running smoothly.

Technical issues

Problems related to technology can usually be divided into ones affecting personal technology and ones affecting shared or provided technology. Issues with personal equipment can often be addressed by the individual, though they may need assistance, while ones relating to shared technologies will generally require specialists to resolve. The important point is to try to think about what might go wrong in advance and work out what you might do instead. This will build resilience into your plans and mean that issues should be easier to resolve because you will not be flustered. A good general practice is to have contact information for helplines and colleagues to hand, as well as an alternative way to contact them, such as a phone, so that if the issue looks serious or long-lasting then you can get support and make sure that the learners are not temporarily left without the guidance of a teacher.

Network/WiFi connections

Probably the most frequently encountered technical issue for both teachers and learners, problems with internet connections can happen to anyone with little warning and can take time to resolve. There are ways to reduce the impact of network issues, but they cannot be completely prevented.

For asynchronous activities, the most effective way to address this issue is to advise the students not to leave participation to the last moment to allow time to seek a solution or find alternative ways to take part. However, the greatest impact will be on synchronous activities, particularly if the issue is affecting the teacher.

To help reduce these impacts:

- position yourself as close to your WiFi router as possible to get a good signal;
- use a wired connection to the router if practical;
- where possible, switch off or limit the use of other WiFi devices in the vicinity during your live session;
- if using a home internet connection, ask other people sharing it not to use too much data during the session, such as by streaming videos or playing online games;
- check the settings in your router to see if you can prioritise your device over others;
- see if you can use your mobile phone's data connection as a temporary WiFi router in case the network drops out completely;
- if a particular person is struggling to get a good connection, such as there is a significant delay in their audio or video, then having them turn off their camera may help;
- if the tool supports it, making another person a co-host will prevent everyone being removed from the session if your connection fails.

Personal equipment failure

While both software and hardware has become more stable in recent years, there always exists the possibility of personal equipment failing. If the failure is with the main device that you use to create materials, run sessions and participate online then in an emergency situation the simplest option is likely to be to use a different device and then resolve the problem with the original device when there is less pressure. If the device is provided to you by your university then you will probably be able to use a support line to help troubleshoot the problem, and in some cases you might also be able to use the same line with personally owned devices.

For issues with devices such as microphones and webcams, here are some things to try:

- test the devices before the taught session to allow time to address any issues;
- check that audio devices are not muted and that the volume is turned up. This is a common problem but is easily fixed. If the volume looks fine on the computer, check whether the audio device has its own mute button;

- unplug and plug the non-functioning device back in again, ideally into a different port if possible. Sometimes cables get jogged loose, and this will make sure that the best possible connection is made;
- if possible, try the microphone or camera device in a different computer. If the problem goes away, then the issue is with the first computer. If it remains then it is likely that the problem is with the device, and replacement may be the best option;
- turn the computer off, wait half a minute or so and turn it back on. Clichéd as this may seem, it often works because it allows the device to start completely fresh without any cumulative issues having formed;
- unplug all other unnecessary devices such as USB drives and printers, reboot, and plug each one back in in turn and test the microphone or camera each time. It may be that something else plugged into your computer is causing a conflict and this will let you identify it;
- remove any software installed just prior to the problem occurring. It may be that a new piece of software is causing problems;
- find out how to configure the relevant settings for your device. These days most USB devices can just be plugged in and out at will, but it might be that your computer has become confused by this and thinks that a device is still plugged in when it is not.

You may find it helpful to provide your students with a checklist like the one above, to help them to test their own equipment.

Local access to tools

In addition to general purpose tools, such as word processer and spreadsheet software, many disciplines have specialist tools that they use extensively and that learners need to use and understand. In face-to-face settings a learner can generally readily access these tools from either a standard computer on campus or in specialist labs; however, this is not possible in online learning. Some ways to address this issue are:

- find out whether the tools can be downloaded for use on personal devices – many universities have agreements with suppliers so that teachers and learners can get access to free copies of required software;
- check whether the university has an alternative way to give remote access to software – there may be a virtual desktop-type system that can be used to access the tools;
- research whether there are alternative free tools that can be used instead – the feasibility of this will depend on how important it is for learners to learn a specific tool rather than the general principles. For example, on the one hand, it may be important that the learners know how to use a specific computer aided design (CAD) tool such as

Autodesk, but, on the other hand, perhaps the teaching can be adjusted to cover general CAD principles that the learners can apply in any CAD tool, including Autodesk;

- investigate whether it is possible for learners to be reimbursed for purchasing important hardware. Physical tools are the hardest to make available in online learning situations, but it might be that the necessary devices can be sent out to the learners or they can claim the cost back from the university. This is more likely to be feasible for relatively generic, low-cost items such as basic graphics tablets for learners on graphic design or mathematics courses, but there may be ways to get other equipment out to learners;

- inform learners about the hardware requirements before they apply to the course to make sure that they are able to afford the necessary equipment and that they buy the right type for the course. For example, make sure that they get a more versatile laptop rather than a limited tablet device.

Web-based access to tools

In contrast to local tools, where one of the main problems is just not having access to the tool off campus, the potential issues around access to online tools such as word processing software, spreadsheets, email apps or cloud storage can be a bit more complex. This is due to the need for an internet connection when using these tools and the variable support that might be available. Some actions to try when encountering a problem are:

- check your email, university IT pages and the tool's main website to see if there is planned or unplanned downtime with the tool and that your account has not expired;

- temporarily disable any unnecessary plugins and extensions in your browser, such as ad blockers;

- try using a different web browser (e.g. if using Chrome try Firefox, or vice versa);

- if you use a university username and password to access it, check that they work with other tools and have not been disabled;

- confirm that your internet connection is working adequately by trying to access a few different websites;

- check that your computer's firewall is not restricting access to the website. How you do this will depend on the computer, so you may need to contact your institution's IT support for advice;

- if the problem relates to a system internal to your university, check whether you need to use a virtual private network (VPN) to access it from outside. Many internal systems have restrictions that prevent access from off campus, but the VPN will make you appear to be on campus;

- find out how you and your learners can access support in using the tool. It may be an officially supported tool that the university IT department will assist with, but it may instead be necessary to contact the provider directly which may take considerably longer.

People issues

The range of potential people issues is broad, so it is only possible to cover some of the most common ones here. Generally, these issues will be harder to resolve, and will likely need to be addressed sensitively and over a longer period.

Inappropriate actions from learners

The seemingly faceless nature of online environments can often lead people to act in ways that they likely wouldn't in a face-to-face situation, such as by making derogatory comments about peers and teachers or deliberately trying to offend others, meaning there may be more issues of this nature than in on-campus delivery. However, in most cases the way that these inappropriate actions are dealt with is the same as it would be face to face. Universities have disciplinary procedures that cover the most extreme situations, and these will apply just as much to online learning as to face-to-face learning. It is worth, therefore, familiarising yourself with these procedures before any problems occur.

For less serious cases, it may be sufficient to speak directly to the learner and explain why their actions were unacceptable and ask them to apologise to the individual or all of their peers as appropriate. Establishing ground rules or a code of conduct, possibly in conjunction with the learners, can help in reducing the occurrence of these problems by making acceptable and unacceptable behaviours explicit at the very start of the course. Figure 10.1 illustrates an example of some guidelines.

E-etiquette rules

Use your real name

Be respectful of others, even when you disagree with what they say

Keep your mic on mute unless asked to turn it on

Engage with all of the activities set

If you're struggling to join in for any reason, please message the Facilitator privately using the Chat function

---

Figure 10.1   An example of e-etiquette rules

Struggling with technology

Many people find technology daunting; this can be the case even when they are accomplished technology users who are having to use an unfamiliar tool. The best way to combat this issue is to introduce new technologies gradually where possible and ensure that there will be sufficient support available for learners and other teachers to learn the tool. Scaffolding the way that people begin to use a tool is an excellent method of making a tool seem less complex as it enables a gradual familiarisation that means that skills and experience build up over time. It is important to give enough time to develop this confidence before a particular tool is used for a high-stakes assessment, otherwise the stress of the required work combined with that of using an unfamiliar tool may be too much for some learners and severely affect their performance. An example might be a new online portfolio tool, where students are supported to upload evidence of their learning in stages, week by week, before a more substantial task is set.

In addition to this gradual introduction there may be services available to assist in developing skills and confidence with particular tools. Many university libraries provide skills development sessions for learners, and sometimes also for teachers, and your learners and you may also have access to online skills development platforms, such as LinkedIn Learning. If such services are not available then it is certainly worth either creating appropriate resources or collating ones that already exist online – YouTube, for example, is an excellent source for tutorial videos on all manner of technologies. Teachers and learners may also be able to get training from their university's library, digital learning, or general IT departments.

Lack of engagement

We have touched upon how to counter a general lack of engagement in previous chapters, and there are multiple potential reasons for this to occur. It may be that the learners are struggling to access the learning materials and activities due to technical barriers or because of the timing of synchronous sessions, or the learners may be becoming fatigued by too many similar activities in quick succession. When this situation arises it is best to get some feedback from both those who are engaging and those that aren't in order to see if there are any common factors that can be addressed – without reducing engagement from those already participating.

Reluctance to engage

Slightly different from the previous issue, there may be some individual learners who are reluctant to engage online. There can be many different reasons why an individual is reluctant to engage, from a general lack of confidence through to lack of support for a specific disability, or external circumstances that make it more difficult for them. The first step here is to identify those learners who may be reluctant and privately discuss the situation with them in a sensitive manner, in particular trying to identify the reason and working out a way that it can be addressed. For example, a shy learner may not want to use their webcam or speak in a large synchronous session with dozens of 'strangers', but may be more comfortable in a small group using a breakout room. In this case it may be possible to develop the learner's confidence by encouraging them to participate more in the small group activities until they feel comfortable speaking to the larger group.

This should all be done sensitively and without pressuring the learners such that it causes them undue stress, and this is where the ground rules mentioned earlier can help to make a more supportive learning environment. It is worth noting that there might be compromises that can be made to accommodate individual learners and encourage their participation. As an example, a learner may be very self-conscious and so not want to turn on their webcam. In this case it could be agreed that this learner is free to turn their camera on and off as they wish, which might allow them more time to get comfortable with their peers and eventually start using the webcam regularly.

Accessibility

We looked at some of the issues around accessibility in Chapter 2, but it is important to remember that these issues might appear at any point during the course, not just at the beginning. For example, a learner may break an arm meaning that it becomes more difficult to type and so get involved in chat during synchronous sessions, in which case you may decide that this particular learner can use their microphone to participate instead. Similarly, a learner may be assessed to have a specific learning difficulty (SpLD), such as dyscalculia, late in the course and adjustments would need to be made from that point on.

Case study

Nicole taught Web Systems Development as part of a Computer Science degree. A key focus in the early part of the course, and one that develops skills used in subsequent modules, is the use of the Structured Query Language (SQL) to create and manipulate databases. When she taught this module face to face it was always in a specialist computer lab where the learners were able to practise on the enterprise-level (and very expensive)

Oracle database platform. However, when planning her delivery of the module online she found out that the university only allowed access to Oracle from this particular computer lab and that it would take several months to allow access from off campus, by which time teaching on the module would already be underway.

While moving the module to a point later in the course would give time for the technical changes to be made, given the fundamental nature of the module this wasn't feasible, so Nicole looked for alternatives to using the university Oracle system. While investigating she found out that a free version of Oracle was available for educational purposes and that it would be suitable for most of her learners. However, there were some who may not be able to run the software because it was not available for their computers. Looking further she found the open source MySQL and MariaDB tools that had broadly equivalent features, would be suitable for all learners and only require some minor changes to her materials.

Nicole adapted her teaching resources to remove anything that was specific to Oracle. She provided information to her online learners about their software options and allowed them to decide which they wanted to use. The sessions ran well, with learners feeling empowered by being able to choose their own tools. In the end, the teaching materials were improved because, by focusing on widely applicable principles rather than the specifics of a single tool, the learners were better able to transfer their skills between database platforms rather than having narrow knowledge of a single platform.

By pre-emptively planning an alternative, Nicole was able to address a potential issue that would have arisen during her teaching and caused significant problems for learners. Offering the learners choice options helped prevent a situation where some learners couldn't take part because they didn't have the 'right' type of laptop, making the module more accommodating to personal choice and the learners' own interests. The approach was so successful that even when the Oracle database was made available externally, Nicole continued to offer this choice to her learners.

REFLECTIVE ACTIVITY

Consider a synchronous session that you intend to run online. What might go wrong and what can you do in advance to reduce the impact of these problems?

If you already have experience of online teaching, think back to a time when things did not go as planned. What could you have done to reduce the impact on your learners?

Reflections

Table 10.1 shows some examples of further problems that may occur in a synchronous session and how these might be responded to.

Table 10.1   Problems and solutions in a synchronous session

Issue	What you could have done in advance?	How you might address it on the spot?
The students cannot access the virtual learning 'room' because you forgot to give them the link or the password.	Send out the link and password prior to the session.\n\nAgree with the students how you will communicate with them outside the live teaching room if needed (such as their university email addresses, through the 'announcement' feature on the virtual learning environment, or via an agreed social media app).	Send out the link and/or password immediately so that students can join in straight away or invite them all by email.\n\nIf you have already agreed how to communicate with students outside the video conferencing platform, they will know where to look for messages from you.
Your camera and mic 'freeze' during a synchronous presentation. You realise your internet connection is unstable.	See the list earlier in this chapter about how to ensure your connection is more reliable.\n\nAgree with your students in advance what will happen if they 'lose' you during a live session. For example, they might wait five minutes and then begin to work on one of the asynchronous tasks in the session folder on the VLE, or you could appoint a co-host who will chair discussions or set tasks in your absence.	In an ideal world you would have a colleague co-teaching with you who could take over if you freeze or disappear.\n\nAlternatively, you could ensure that a colleague is on standby to be contacted by telephone should you need to call on them to step in.\n\nIf you have agreed a plan with your students for this eventuality, you can relax in the knowledge that they know what to do while they're waiting for you to come back online.
You try to put the students into pre-arranged groups in the breakout rooms, but it is taking you longer than anticipated and you're getting flustered.	Make a list before the session showing who is in which group.\n\nDepending on the tool you are using, you might be able to set them up in advance so that when you're ready to use them, all you need do is press a button. However, it may be that you want to start with random groups and then use pre-arranged groups later in the session. If this is the case, plan in a break to give you time to set the rooms up.	Suggest to the students that they take a five- to ten-minute comfort break while you sort out the breakout rooms. Breaks are always welcome, and in fact are good practice when sitting in front of a screen for long periods.

(Continued)

Table 10.1   (Continued)

Issue	What you could have done in advance?	How you might address it on the spot?
You set up a task for the students such as using an online message board or taking part in an online quiz, and it does not work.	Test out whatever tool you are going to use and make sure that the activities are not time limited. You may not have realised that the students have to set up their own accounts with the tool that you're using before they can access it, so would need to have them do this before the session. You can also plan back-up activities just in case.	Call a three-minute break while you establish a new link to the tool that the students are going to use. Otherwise, invent an alternative task on the spot. If you were going to use a message board, ask the students to type into the 'chat' function instead. If you were going to use a quiz, read out the questions 'live' and get the students to write down the answers.
A student has a problem with her microphone and is virtually inaudible. You ask her to use the chat function instead, as a temporary measure, but she insists on continuing to use the mic. The other students begin to get frustrated.	Prior to the start of the course of module, instruct the students to carry out their own equipment check and provide links to helpdesk support should they experience any problems. Direct students who are not confident in using the equipment to the appropriate support team – for example, to be shown how to adjust the volume on their microphone. Include guidance on this issue in the group 'ground rules', e.g. if your mic malfunctions, be prepared to use the chat function until the issue is resolved.	Repeat the request for the student to use the chat function. If this does not work, call a break and then speak to the student one to one (e.g. by phone). Provide alternative access to the synchronous session. Some video conferencing tools provide telephone numbers to enable users to access the session by phone. As a last resort, the teacher can generally mute the microphone of session participants, giving the opportunity to move on before the rest of the learners become too frustrated.
The students are getting tired and feeling overloaded, but because you are not in each other's physical presence, it is hard for you to pick this up.	Plan regular breaks. Incorporate a variety of activities. Encourage students to get up and move around and have refreshments. Be realistic about how much you can 'cover' in a single synchronous session. Convert some of the content into asynchronous activities that can be completed prior to or following the synchronous session.	Check in regularly with the students as to how they're feeling – invite them to make a comment in the chat or use the 'thumbs up' sign if they're happy to carry on, or even to indicate to the camera their current state of mind (you may have to stop screen-sharing to see everyone's faces). You can also conduct a quick poll to see who is ready for a break or not.

Careful preparation and managing student expectations can go a long way towards preventing difficulties from occurring in synchronous sessions. However, flexibility, imagination and the willingness to improvise can also help too. Above all, investing time in building up a good relationship with your students means that if things do go wrong, they will trust you to sort it out and know that you have their best interests at heart.

Further reading

Brown, J. (2020) 5 best practices for managing virtual breakout rooms. *EdTech Magazine*. 10 November. Available online at: https://edtechmagazine.com/k12/article/2020/11/5-best-practices-managing-virtual-breakout-rooms (accessed 14 November 2020).

Some interesting ways of using virtual breakout rooms with students to maximise engagement and accessibility.

Coogan, J. (2019) E-resources troubleshooting and user support at a primarily distance learning/online higher education institution: current practice and future considerations. *Journal of Electronic Resources Librarianship*, 31(3), 180–8.

The story of how a university library developed web-based technical help pages to support its worldwide cohort of students.

Gillett-Swan, J. (2017) The challenges of online learning supporting and engaging the isolated learner. *Journal of Learning Design*, 10(1), 20–30.

A look at the problems in adopting a 'one-size-fits-all' approach to online learning.

Hardy, L. (2017) *The A–Z of Online Teaching Challenges*. Elearning Industry. Available online at: https://elearningindustry.com/online-teaching-challenges-a-z (accessed 14 November 2020).

An easy to read quick guide to issues that can occur in online teaching, which includes a helpful focus on self-care for teachers.

Karkar-Esperat, T. (2018) International graduate students' challenges and learning experiences in online classes. *Journal of International Students*, 8(4), 1722–35.

Analysis of some of the barriers to learning experienced by international students enrolled on an online course.

Lehman, R. and Conceição, S. (2015) *Motivating and Retaining Online Students: Research-Based Strategies that Work* (1st edn). San Francisco: Jossey-Bass.

This book outlines some approaches for improving student engagement in online learning.

INDEX

5C Framework 27

A Beautiful Mind 109
AbilityNet 16–17
academic resource curation 29
accessibility
  alternative formats 15–16
  asynchronous learning 75
  checking 16
  dictation 15
  legislative drive 12
  SCULPT model 12–14
  tools 14–15
  video 14
Accessibility checker 16
active learning 66–7
Adobe Connect 28
Adobe Spark 31
animated videos 51
annotated bibliographies 88
annotations 95–6
assessment
  asynchronous sessions 79–80
  case study 98
  feedback 95–8
  formative and summative 87–8
  inclusive and feedback 99
  types of 88–93
asynchronous sessions
  additional support or extension
    opportunities 80–1
  assessment 79–80
  collaborative or individual tasks 78–9
  design considerations 80–1
  planning and preparation 76–80
  presentation slides 76–7
  pros and cons 75
  sliding flaws case study 82–4
  task instructions 78
  terminology 5
  tools 76–7
audio commentary 52
audio feedback 96
audio podcasts 53
audits of students' readiness 63

automated feedback 97
avatars 104–5

Beckingham, S. 27
Beetham, H. 5, 23
bespoke videos 51
Blackboard Ally 15, 16
Blackboard Collaborate 28, 30
blended learning terminology 4
Blogger 31
blogs 31

Canva 31
chunked slides 59–60
collaborating 29–30
colorblinding 16
comic book endings 105–6
communicating tools 28
computer aided design (CAD) 115–16
computer games 104–7
connecting tools 27–8
constructivism 50
course community 44–5
creating 30–1
critiques 88
curating 29

decolonising the curriculum 19
defamiliarising the familiar 107–9
demonstrations/walkthroughs 89
depression 55
design science 2
designing online teaching and
  learning 5–7
dictation 15
Diffusion of Innovation model 24
digital capability 17–18
digital learning terminology 4
digital technologies 5
discussion boards 28
discussion forums 53
dissertations/projects 89
distance learning terminology 5
diversity 12
document creation 29–30

e-etiquette rules 117
enactments 108
engagement 118–19
environment 43–4 *see also* accessibility
essay writing case study 82–4
essays 89–90
exams 91, 92
expectations 3

face-to-face learning
    adapting for online 6–7
    linear approach 37–8
    terminology 4
feedback
    active learning and 66–7
    role of 94–5
    types of 95–8
flexibility 3
food and mood 54–6
food and mood case study 56–9
formative assessment 87–8

gamification 106–7
Google Drive 30

Hockings, C. 12

in-session quizzes 90
inappropriate actions 117
inclusivity *see also* accessibility
    other considerations 17–20
    overview 12
infographics 53
information-application structure 35, 36
Information-focused Learning 26
Instagram 28
interviews 90
isolation 6

JAWS 15

Kahoot 30

lack of engagement 118
laggardism 24
Laurillard, D. 2, 5
learning activities 40
learning barista 39–43
learning logs 43
learning units 40
Learning units, Activities, Timing, Tools and
    Environment (LATTE) 39–43
    case study 45–6
lecture capture 50–1
LinkedIn 28
live feedback 97–8

macro level 38–9
macro, meso and micro levels 36
marking grids/rubrics 96
massive open online course (MOOC) 39
media outputs 30–1
Mendeley 29
mental health 54–6
Mentimeter 30
mentoring 45
meso level 37–8
micro level 36–7
Microsoft 365 30
Microsoft Sway 31
Microsoft Teams 30
module structures 37–8
motivation 3

Nash, J. 109
Nerantzi, C. 27
network/wi-fi connections 113–14
non-linear approach 37–8
nutrition module case study 53
NVDA 15

off the shelf videos 51
on-campus 4
online learning
    advantages of 5–6
    challenges of 6
    research 3
    terminology 4
online tests 90
open-book exams 91
opportunities 35–9
Oracle 119–20
oral exams 92

PDF files 16
PebblePad 31
peer-support 45
people issues 117–19
personal curation 29
personal equipment failures 114–15
pets, places, children and washing
        machines 107–8
planning and preparation 8
poetry 102
portfolios 31, 43, 91
posters 91
Powtoon 30, 51
pre-recorded videos 51
presentation slides
    adapting for online 56–60
    case study 56–9
    chunked slides 59–60
    food and mood case study 54–6

self-access slides 53, 59
self-directed 76–7
presentations
    assessment 91–2
    other ways 53–6
    synchronous teaching 67–8
    in video format 50–3
prior knowledge and experience 19
professional presence 27–8
project assessments 89, 92
project communication 30
Puentedura, R.R. 40

questions 53
quizzes 53, 90

reluctance to engage 118–19
research into online learning 3
research methods module scheme 37–8
research/project proposals 92
resource availability 17
Rogers, E. 24
role-play 108
rubrics 96

scavenger hunts 103
screen readers 14–15
screencast feedback 96
screencast-o-matic 31
SCULPT model 12–14
self-access slides 59
Sharpe, R. 5, 23
Sheffield Hallam University 25
showcases 31
Slack 30
social anxiety 20
social curation 29
social media 18, 27
social presence 3, 8
sound files 53
staffing 64–5
stories 108
Structured Query Language (SQL) 119–20
structuring case study 45–6
student-led presentations 51
Substitution–Augmentation–Modification–
    Redefinition model (SAMR) 40
summative assessment 87–8
SWOT analysis case study 7–8
synchronous sessions
    active learning and feedback 66–7
    facilitating 68–72
    international seminars 68–9
    jigsaw discussion case study 70–2
    planning and preparation 64–9
    presenting 67–8

pros and cons 63–4
staffing 64–5
terminology 5
timing and breaks 65–6
tools 63–4
vs asynchronous 41–3

teacher-centric approach 35
Teaching Approaches Menu (Sheffield
    Hallam University) 25
technical issues 113–17
techno-determinism 23–4
technology
    case study 119–20
    struggles with 118
    thinking pedagogically 24–5
terminology 4–5
tests 90
The Matrix 50
theory and practice case study 82–4
thinking holistically 44–5
time, prioritising 8
time zones 18
timing 65–6
timing of units 40–1
tools
    case study 31–2
    laggardism 24
    local access to 115–16
    preferences 41–3
    techno-determinism 23–4
    terminology 23
    thinking pedagogically 24–5
    types of 27–31
    web-based access 116–17
trouble-shooting
    case study 119–20
    e-etiquette rules 117
    engagement 118–19
    inappropriate actions 117
    local access to tools 115–16
    network/wi-fi connections 113–14
    people issues 117–19
    personal equipment failures 114–15
    problems and solutions 121–3
    technical issues 113–17
tutors, challenging 19

video accessibility 14
video conferencing/webinar 28
video feedback 97
video presentations 50–3
video techniques 52–3
virtual reality (VR) 23
viva/oral exams 92
voting/polling 30

warm-ups 102–4
Web Content Accessibility
    Guidelines 12
web-literacy 3
wi-fi connections 113–14
Wiki-race 102–3
Wilson, S. 108

windows, walls and tablecloths 109
WordPress 31
work and family commitments 18–19
written comments 95

Zoom 28, 30
Zotero 29